Provoke

FROM THE BESTSELLING TEAM THAT
BROUGHT YOU *DETONATE*

Provoke

How Leaders
Shape the Future
by Overcoming
Fatal Human Flaws

GEOFF TUFF
STEVEN GOLDBACH

ILLUSTRATIONS BY TOM FISHBURNE

WILEY

Published by John Wiley & Sons, Inc., Hoboken, New Jersey.
Published simultaneously in Canada.

No part of this publication may be reproduced, stored in a retrieval system, or
transmitted in any form or by any means, electronic, mechanical, photocopying,
recording, scanning, or otherwise, except as permitted under Section 107 or 108 of
the 1976 United States Copyright Act, without either the prior written permission
of the Publisher, or authorization through payment of the appropriate per-copy fee
to the Copyright Clearance Center, Inc., 222 Rosewood Drive, Danvers, MA 01923,
(978) 750-8400, fax (978) 646-8600, or on the Web at www.copyright.com. Requests
to the Publisher for permission should be addressed to the Permissions Department,
John Wiley & Sons, Inc., 111 River Street, Hoboken, NJ 07030, (201) 748-6011, fax
(201) 748-6008, or online at http://www.wiley.com/go/permissions.

Limit of Liability/Disclaimer of Warranty: While the publisher and author have used
their best efforts in preparing this book, they make no representations or warranties
with respect to the accuracy or completeness of the contents of this book and
specifically disclaim any implied warranties of merchantability or fitness for a
particular purpose. No warranty may be created or extended by sales representatives
or written sales materials. The advice and strategies contained herein may not be
suitable for your situation. You should consult with a professional where appropriate.
Neither the publisher nor author shall be liable for any loss of profit or any other
commercial damages, including but not limited to special, incidental, consequential,
or other damages.

For general information on our other products and services or for technical support,
please contact our Customer Care Department within the United States at (800)
762-2974, outside the United States at (317) 572-3993 or fax (317) 572-4002.

Wiley publishes in a variety of print and electronic formats and by print-on-demand.
Some material included with standard print versions of this book may not be
included in e-books or in print-on-demand. If this book refers to media such as a CD
or DVD that is not included in the version you purchased, you may download this
material at http://booksupport.wiley.com. For more information about Wiley
products, visit www.wiley.com.

Library of Congress Cataloging-in-Publication Data

Names: Tuff, Geoff, 1970- author. | Goldbach, Steve, 1973- author.
Title: Provoke : how leaders shape the future by overcoming fatal human
   flaws / Geoff Tuff, Steven Goldbach.
Description: Hoboken, New Jersey : Wiley, [2021] | Includes index.
Identifiers: LCCN 2021020639 (print) | LCCN 2021020640 (ebook) | ISBN
   9781119764472 (cloth) | ISBN 9781119787556 (adobe pdf) | ISBN
   9781119787549 (epub)
Subjects: LCSH: Leadership.
Classification: LCC HD57.7 .T865 2021 (print) | LCC HD57.7 (ebook) | DDC
   658.4/092—dc23
LC record available at https://lccn.loc.gov/2021020639
LC ebook record available at https://lccn.loc.gov/2021020640

Back Cover Cartoon: © Tom Fishburne
Cover design: Paul McCarthy
SKY10028517_072721

For our families: Martha, Michelle, our kids, our siblings, and especially our parents, who originally provoked us to look at the world inquisitively.

CONTENTS

INTRODUCTION

Kids love rollercoasters.

Not all kids, and not all rollercoasters . . . but by and large they just love them.

Although they exhibit patience for nothing else, they are willing to wait in a long line just to get a few minutes of thrill. They smile with glee as the car grinds and clacks up the track at a snail's pace, anticipating the hair-raising freefall that comes on the other side when all that potential energy is converted to kinetic. Many of them even put up their hands as the car moves from one phase to the next to increase the thrill level, testing the safety design of the harness that is keeping them inside. Not knowing precisely what's coming doesn't scare them. It excites them.

In adulthood, it's safe to say one's relationship with rollercoasters changes. There are some who still love them, but our (albeit unscientific) experience suggests it becomes a smaller and smaller proportion of the population as we age. For those who do not enjoy rollercoasters, the thrill is gone and the experience is quite literally the opposite of the glee of youth. Instead of eyes wide open, looking around at the world and what's to come, the eyes stay clamped shut in the hope that not seeing will make the experience less painful. Instead of testing the boundaries of the safety system by raising your arms, riders freeze in place, white-knuckling the safety bar, fingernails dug in, just praying for a return to stable ground. Instead of seeing what happens, these riders wish for a mental map of what's coming next and desperately hope that the whole thing will just end as quickly as possible.

The physical experience is the same – the feel of the car, the path of the track, and the centripetal force bolstered by redundant safety mechanisms. But the emotional reaction to the experience is fundamentally different.

The history of leadership is chock-full of people who look like both types of riders: those who embrace the ride and others whose fixation on each possible pitfall renders them immobile. Both groups, in past decades, have had a reliable foundation on which to "ride," with predictable outcomes linked either to carefree confidence that everything is on a safe path or obsessive overanalysis of knowable details. But the plight of each archetype is complicated by the realities of today's environment, which are serving up increasingly unpredictable twists, crests, and dives.

Whether their bias has been to follow the momentum of past experience or to call for ever-increasing burdens of analytical proof, leaders will have a harder and harder time anticipating and capitalizing on the peaks. Yet it's at these peaks when new opportunities shift from the possibility of "if" to the inevitability of "when." Past data and experience are proving less useful and, to make matters worse, most leaders (whether they know it or not) are forced to act with blinders on. Basic human cognitive biases – what we call "fatal flaws" – narrow individual and organizational peripheral vision and lead to all-too-typical dysfunction.

The best leaders rise above these constraints to gain perspective; they set aside their terror of the ride and summon their inner child, who can better deal with the twists and turns. They recognize – and even appreciate – that while they may not be able to control all the outcomes, they can plan for and control their reactions.

These days, the conviction to act – especially in the absence of perfect data – is the only way to provoke the future you desire. Action creates potential energy. Action allows you to position yourself to see the peak sooner and more clearly than others. Action gives you the power to move through the phase change of "if" to "when" so that you can make the most use of the kinetic energy when it's released.

And action, in an uncertain world, is increasingly the best way to learn. If you don't act with purpose, your once-thriving business could suddenly become a "wind-down" firm, operating on borrowed time.

Detonate, our previous book, was our call to selectively blow up the foundations of past success to allow for forward progress. *Provoke* is about looking forward and working through the natural human instincts that keep people frozen in place, thinking and analyzing. It is about forcefully gathering the will to act in the face of deepening uncertainty and DO SOMETHING!

PART I

PREDICTABLE PATTERNS

CHAPTER 1

Patterns from the Past

"1.75%? Why would I care?" asked the senior executive as he flippantly tossed the PowerPoint page onto his conference table, put his foot on the table, leaned back in his chair, and, yes, stuck his hand into his pants like Al Bundy in the 1990s sitcom *Married with Children*.

Steve and his colleague exchanged a knowing glance. They had worked together for 15 years and by that point they basically shared a brain, which, at that point, was thinking: "Is this guy for real?"

They were in his lavish office, sitting at his conference table. Steve noticed the golf trophies, pictures with celebrities, and large and expensive desk. The office screamed, "I'm successful!"

It was 2009 and, given the difficult economic climate, Steve and his colleague were being especially aggressive in getting out to meet new executives. They had done some work for a large, diversified media and communications company, creating a segmentation of consumer behavior in its industry. Their client, pleased with the work, was looking to present it at an upcoming industry conference and wanted to get some reactions from executives at peer companies – hence the reason they were sitting in Al Bundy's office.

The work they were sharing included a detailed segmentation of the consumer landscape for communications services like Internet, phone, video/television packages, and security. They had surveyed thousands of customers about their behaviors and actions. The survey revealed the typical and expected results: when people got married or had families, their Internet and video usage dramatically changed from when they were single. Expenditure on things like pay-per-view and other channels tended to be higher among this group. With more devices in the house, they also were willing to pay for higher Internet bandwidth.

This wasn't news. Companies in this space knew and loved these customers. They paid their bills on time, they didn't move, and as a result they didn't "churn." And, back in 2009, they probably had a landline, too. Therefore, if you successfully acquired one of these customers, you were likely to retain them, leading to a steady, predictable stream of revenue.

At the other end of the spectrum were the singles. They typically lived in an apartment and had more focused communications needs. This was a group that tended to select the most basic Internet and television packages. Sometimes this choice was driven by personal preference (think people who like to read at night). But sometimes this was driven by affordability, where having lots of channels could be expensive. You could predict the reasons for this choice based on income levels (typically tied to specific geographic locations) and whether the home was rented or owned. Some singles with higher disposable income bought a more comprehensive communications package, but it typically included just video and Internet; even in 2009, this group didn't want a landline – a mobile phone was just fine for them. These singles, perhaps because of their income or preferences, were willing to spend more on faster Internet speeds and specialty channels.

Because of the high capital intensity of the communications and entertainment distribution market, players in this industry wanted to win *all* of these customers. It wasn't economically viable to focus on just one segment, so Steve's work was designed to help companies customize their product, pricing, and marketing messages to better target the needs of each of these groups. For instance, if you had an area that overindexed on owned homes, that was a sign that there were probably a lot of families with kids, and you'd advertise a comprehensive package. If you were targeting an urban area with a lot of apartment renters, you'd make different choices.

None of this was particularly earth-shattering in 2009. The work was solid, but the patterns were generally predictable to experienced executives in the space.

Except for one small anomaly.

A seemingly inconsequential group of customers – that 1.75% that the exec had dismissed – was exhibiting some unique behaviors that made it challenging to assign them to one of the larger segments. When segmenting an industry, it's preferential to get to between four and eight meaningful segments of the marketplace that are small enough to be unique but large enough to merit individual focus. But, from an analytical perspective, the 1.75% just didn't fit into any segment.

These were younger people, so Steve and his team tried to type them to the segment with other single people. But they didn't really fit. They had lower income, so the team tried to group them with the budget-conscious single group, but they didn't pick the lowest-cost Internet. They actually wanted high Internet speeds. They tried to bundle them with the higher-income single people, but those folks didn't buy TV packages. Most of the time they would pick the most basic TV package, and many of them didn't even have a TV package at all. If they could buy "just Internet," they would – but at high speeds.

If their Internet provider required them to also purchase television or phone, they might purchase Internet elsewhere, sometimes getting a cellular hotspot (previously you could just use your mobile phone as a hotspot) instead of a wired home connection.

When Steve and his team further investigated this group and tried to understand whether they were just uninterested in video content, they found the opposite. This cohort of singles was quite interested in video content, but they weren't watching traditional network programming. They watched short-form videos on the then-new YouTube. They watched snippets of online video and they subscribed to the new streaming service offered by Netflix, introduced a year earlier, which had only around 1,000 titles and set a limit of 18 hours of streaming per month, a far cry from the Netflix that has become both a noun and a verb.[1]

Intrigued, Steve and his team dug deeper. What they found was that this behavior was rooted in preferences, not cost: this small group simply preferred to consume content in this way. The segment wanted to watch the shows they wanted to watch when they wanted to watch them. They wanted smaller, bite-sized chunks of content. They wanted it ad-free (but, given that they were budget constrained, they would tolerate ads if that helped make it more affordable). And they were pretty agile about finding ways to view their favorite shows online without paying for them, if it could be done.

In short, they consumed content in this way not because it was *cheaper* but because it was *better* – although the fact that it was also cheaper made it a zero-trade-off change for consumers.

But the executive wasn't buying it. He seemed more interested in discrediting the research methodology than the findings.

Remind me, how many people were in your study?

How did you weight your sample?

Did you conduct this study nationally or regionally?

Was the survey conducted online or on the phone?

After glancing at his colleague, Steve asked, "Are you curious to learn more about the behavior of this group of customers? It seems as though if the group became more prominent, it would challenge the way you make money."

It was at that point the executive responded with his *why would I care* response and arrogantly stuck his hand in his pants.

The behavior of this executive is part of a pattern that we have observed time and time again with leaders of all kinds – and it's one of the core reasons we wrote *Provoke*. When an anomaly emerges in their space, something that might be important, the vast majority of humans behave in a persistently predictable pattern. It's as if executives are riding that roller-coaster but fail to recognize that they are in fact going up a steep slope that will at some point tip over into the ride of their lives – and not in a good way. The potential of the trend – if it *might* happen – shifts to when it *will* happen. Too many executives fail to anticipate that phase change. They:

Miss the trend

Deny the trend

Analyze the trend

Respond meekly to the trend

MISS THE TREND

The first issue that people seem to have is that they don't even see things that are happening under their noses. In the case of the cord-cutting behavior described above, the consulting team might have missed it themselves if there had not already been some reporting of the then-fringe behavior. But they also had the benefit of having a team of young people, many of whom were themselves contemplating cutting the cord because they simply could not understand why anyone would want to pay for something that forced them to watch a show at a scheduled time versus when it was convenient for them.

In general, we miss trends not because we aren't looking, but because our brain processes the raw data of what we see through an unconscious filter of our own experiences. Unless you consciously learn how to turn that filter off, it can be hard to see something right in front of your nose.[2]

DENY THE TREND

"1.75%. Why would I care?" The preceding experience with the executive is an example of denial. Denial can take many forms.

Steve saw a subtler form of denial, which was to question and discredit the observation. We've seen with other trends (e.g., humans' impact on climate, vaccines) that denial can include just an outright refutation of the findings. But after missing something for a long time, having it pointed out to you frequently sparks a negative response and deniers will dig in. The lesson? People don't like to be shown they have missed something important.

(OVER)ANALYZE THE TREND

After a period of denial, some will turn to analysis. Executives will start to ask lots of questions about how big it is, how fast it's moving, how many people it will impact. And there are meetings . . . so many meetings . . . and all with their requisite PowerPoint decks. We frequently find that some analysis leads to more analysis. The more you look at something, the more you find other ways you could look at it. This is all designed, of course, to give executives more specificity on the problem (or opportunity) their business faces. Rarely do we see meetings that focus on analysis end with a decision to take action in the market; most of the time, the conclusion is that the action required is to go do more analysis.

RESPOND MEEKLY TO THE TREND

Sadly, in the rare cases where we do see executives take action – after an unduly long period of study – it's often too little, too late. Just think about the efforts of brick-and-mortar department stores to respond to the long curve of the online shopping trend. Instead of making deliberate choices to make what we call "minimally viable moves" in the face of early signals, they instead waited for evidence of the trend to hit them in the face and then had market forces dictate their path forward. There's often a theoretical debate in boardrooms about whether to pursue a "first mover" or "fast follower" strategy. Unfortunately, the fast follower position is almost always framed as "wait for someone to be successful in the marketplace to *get started*." This is a choice that is increasingly doomed to failure given the degree to which markets are becoming more "winner take all." And, let's face it, most "fast followers" are really dawdlers.[3]

This pattern of behavior, which we've seen over and over again, prompted us to write *Provoke*. There are many trends we see in our line of work as strategists and consultants that are labeled as "uncertain." A chasm separates *if* something will happen (what we think of as true uncertainty) from the uncertainty of *when* something will happen. This difference matters immensely. It dictates how you act in the face of the trend, and the failure to recognize this nuance in meaning is what leads most leaders to miss, deny, analyze, and respond meekly, following the pattern of our hand-in-his-waistband executive.

THE SOLUTION IS TO *PROVOKE*

Our executive, and the organization he represented, had blinders on – blinders that we all wear, to one extent or another – that narrowed its organizational peripheral vision and ability to evaluate the importance of the changes found on the periphery. These blinders – constructed of basic human biases that we all share – mean that the playing fields we observe are narrower than the real world. Our maps, as the saying goes, are not the territory.

Combined with organizational dysfunction – overanalysis; meetings with no end or, seemingly, any point; and so on – they lead to systematic inaction. That inaction means that rather than setting our own course, we let others make decisions for us or limit the range of our choices – just as brick-and-mortar stores did. Our momentum (really, our inertia) will drag us into a predictable series of choices that will lead to failure in the face of a new reality represented by the glimmer of those trends.

These biases are the subject of the chapters of Part I, Predictable Patterns. We also offer solutions you can start implementing now to overcome some of these issues.

In Part II, Principles of Provocation, we introduce five moves you can make depending on whether you face an "if" or a "when." These are: envision the future, position yourself for success, drive change, adapt to changing circumstances, and activate your ecosystem. These tools will help you avoid those biases that prevent meaningful action, expand your peripheral vision to better assess your playing field, and prompt you to actually DO SOMETHING!

Some people are more successful at circumventing the problems caused by our biases. In Part III, Profiles of Provocateurs, we present three stories – inspirational ones, we think – of executives who have provoked their organizations to create a better future.

But first let's return to our friend with his hand down his pants and perhaps a bit of egg on his face today now that we're all cord cutters. Steve and his colleague were unable that day to convince him to take an interest in that small group. It remained, at least on that afternoon in his fancy office, too small a segment to matter. We don't know if or how much his company debated the idea later, but it's fair to characterize their market responses as meek relative to Netflix's. They were too late to catch up (although we're sure they thought of themselves as fast followers). It took them a while to get around to taking action, despite already having many of the requisite capabilities within their organization.

In the meantime, Netflix's stock price (adjusted for splits) has gone from roughly $4 at the beginning of 2008 at the time of the meeting to over $500 at the time of our writing this, an increase of more than 100-fold. At the end of Q3 in 2020, Netflix was approaching 200 million paying members (the last published statistic at the time of writing) and had a market capitalization in excess of $200 billion.

At the same time, the executive team at our client (who introduced us to the person in the story) followed a different strategy. Based on their early insight into this trend, they realized they were now effectively a *wind-down firm*. A wind-down firm is a cousin of the *pop-up firm*, which itself is launched to capture a narrow window of market demand – think of a Halloween store that pops up on October 1 and disappears on November 1. The difference is that the wind-down firm had as its original intent the goal to "last forever," but is now riding the wave to obsolescence whether its executives know it or not.

Because of their early insight, our client realized that, without meaningful reinvention, their business model was dead, despite still being highly profitable. So they sold the business. The choice to sell was ultimately a good one for them. They were able to cash out in time, whereas companies with similar assets, capabilities, and business models continue to struggle with the growing segment of customers that prefers to have more control over their content experience through companies like Netflix.

While choosing to become a wind-down firm is a completely legitimate strategy choice, there is a lot of potential value creation in adapting and successfully pursuing new market trends. That's what we want to explore with *Provoke*: as leaders, we all need to have better pattern recognition capability to enable us to spot trends and move to where the world is going to be. Even if you ultimately decide not to pursue the trend, the moves we describe will ensure you are making that decision on your terms and not those dictated by market forces.

But before we get into how to spot those trends, we need to identify – and correct for – the fatal human flaws that get in the way of us seeing these trends in the first place. In Chapter 2, we'll address how to go from "ifs" to "whens" – that is, how to stop treating trends that are already unfolding as mere possibilities.

Chapter 2

On the Importance of "If" versus "When"

Daddy, I used the "Dude Wipes" and my tushy feels minty.

—*Grayson Goldbach, age 5, during the great toilet
paper shortage of March 2020*

Before the pandemic, you probably took toilet paper for granted. And reasonably so. It's one of many things that we use every day without much conscious thought. It's something we just assume will be there for us – until it's not. That's when people go into a mini-panic. Remember the episode from the television show, *Seinfeld*, where the antagonist du jour told Elaine, "I don't have a square to spare"? The pandemic gave us a window into how humans would behave if a TP shortage were an ongoing challenge.

We believe human behavior is the most basic "subatomic element" of business. The pandemic gave us many opportunities to observe human behavior under periods of severe disruption. And it turns out that, when faced with such massive disruption, toilet paper is one of the things that helps people feel secure when on hand in large quantities. We also learned that people really have no idea how much toilet paper they actually need . . . so much so that in early 2020, a plethora of toilet paper calculator sites suddenly started to pop up on

Internet ad feeds – something neither of us had imagined needing before.

The combination of fear and poor estimation led to some pretty interesting hoarding behavior and a resultant run on toilet paper. Rational or not, it was most certainly the case that when you went to buy TP it was difficult to find.

Before getting into this any further, let's just be clear – we are going to devote a fair bit of Chapter 2 to the behaviors around, well, Number 2. Why must we talk about something that makes everyone just a slight bit uncomfortable? This was the best example of something that literally everyone must do, and, as it turns out, there were many new and interesting ways people dealt with the potential shortage. And new and interesting human behaviors are the building blocks of opportunity.

In one instance, we saw consumers leverage technology to make the sharing of toilet paper simpler. One such instance was captured on film in San Francisco, the technology hub of the world, where a person flew a drone to a friend who was in need. (It's worth the reading break to watch the video here: https://mashable.com/article/drone-delivery-toilet-paper-san-francisco-coronavirus/.) Could you imagine this as a business at scale? Instead of ride sharing, imagine a local TP sharing service with delivery-on-demand via drones. Maybe not. In another instance, we saw South Carolina police handing out toilet paper instead of tickets as a gesture of goodwill at the start of the pandemic.[1]

As it turns out, though, the need for actual toilet paper is not the issue. It's the *fear* of being without toilet paper that leads to hoarding behavior. We wish we could say we were "enlightened consumers" and didn't hoard, but we'd be lying. We freaked out, too. Steve did the grocery shopping in his household during the pandemic (a behavior that stuck as the initial lockdowns lifted) and was instructed to buy whatever toilet paper he could find on *every* trip. His family ordered commercial-grade toilet paper with a delivery date of six weeks out, just in case. They even ordered a brand of wet toilet paper they could find online for quicker delivery: "Dude Wipes."

In times of dramatic change, humans are known to change habits, which can lead to permanent behavior change. At the time of writing, it's not yet clear what new habits will stick once we emerge from the pandemic, but it is clear that many long-standing habits will be challenged. A greater proportion of people will certainly be able to work remotely on a more frequent basis, even when there is return to office work. People will likely pay more attention to frequent handwashing. And maybe people will continue to make sourdough regularly at home.

Habits are a critical underpinning to businesses. Think of all the brands that you buy all the time without thinking – including, most likely, your brand of milk, your laundry detergent, and your deodorant. You probably have a habit around your morning coffee, whether you make it at home, pick it up at a basic local coffee shop, or pay premium prices from national retailers. And, until you read this last paragraph, you probably didn't think about it much.[2]

During the pandemic, many of these habits were challenged. For both of us, used to getting "our coffee on the outside" (to quote another *Seinfeld* line), we had to adapt during the lockdown. Geoff returned to getting his coffee on the outside as businesses opened up, while Steve is more than happy to continue to brew his own, having become proficient at making coffee with a French press. As sticky as they are, when habits do change, they impact businesses considerably.

So, given the magnitude of the challenge, did we see a shift in the market for toilet paper or substitutes? As it turns out – yes! A small group of consumers made the decision to no longer be beholden to toilet paper supply. They installed bidets in their homes.

Lest we be accused of only paying attention to the U.S. market, we should acknowledge that bidets are commonplace in many countries around the world, even mandatory. In Italy, for example, a 1975 hygiene law requires bidets to be in at least one household bathroom. In Asia, a company named Toto brought bidets into the digital age with electronic control panels and became a staple in Japanese homes. And then in March 2020, sales of bidets rose dramatically in the United States. Some companies saw sales peak at more than 10 times normal volume.[3]

The critical question this raises – for paper supply companies, for white goods manufacturers, and for consumers looking to move when prices are right – is whether this shift is a one-time blip in sales or a more permanent trend toward the use of bidets among Americans.

Let's leave the bathroom behind for a moment and generalize the concept that we are going to examine for the remainder of the book. Broadly, there are two phases of any trend, each characterized by the nature of the uncertainty around the trend. In the initial "if" stage, it's still uncertain if the trend will come to fruition; in the "when" stage, the trend has progressed, gathered momentum, and crossed an important inflection point where it's no longer uncertain whether it will come to fruition. It's only a question of when and, sometimes, to what extent.

Our core hypothesis for this book is that once an "if" becomes a "when," the nature of a leader's response must change. The opportunity is to focus on the moves you can make that will shape the trend to create a better future – one where your organization is advantaged.

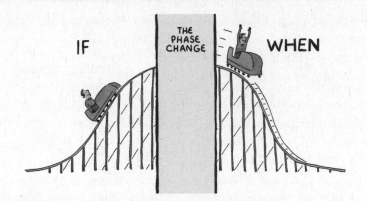

The "if-to-when" shift is, as we wrote in the Introduction, similar to a rollercoaster. That big initial climb as a cable pulls the car up the hill is the "if" stage. The rollercoaster cars are building up a ton of potential energy, and if they stop, they might just slide backwards. But when the cars get to the peak and start to tip, that potential energy becomes kinetic and the momentum takes the cars through loops, twists, and turns, seemingly with a life of their own. Once you hit that inflection point, the "when" stage kicks in. During this transition – something we call the "phase change" – the critical question is how long it will take for the trend to resolve into inevitability.

While it's impossible to be exhaustive about all the mechanisms that might be at play in moving from "if" to "when" (human behavior is admittedly more complicated than the physics of rollercoasters), we like to lean on something from the world of design-driven innovation called the "Balanced Breakthrough Model." The basic notion behind this model is that a "balanced" innovation that has more likelihood of succeeding in the market will simultaneously build in aspects of desirability (the market wants it), feasibility (the innovator can produce it), and viability (the innovator can eventually make money from it). Similarly, a trend that seems headed in the direction of checking all three of these boxes has a much higher likelihood of passing through the phase change to "when" than other, less robust trends.[4]

The most critical aspect of desirability is the degree to which the trend has an unequivocally better outcome than the current state. If the endpoint of the trend is better for all customers on every dimension relative to what exists today, then it's only a matter of when it will take off. That assumes it is or becomes feasible and someone figures out the right business model to make money from it . . . but we're strong believers in almost anything being possible if the right demand conditions are in place. If the improvement is only marginal or only meaningful to a small proportion of the population, then feasibility or viability needs to be off the charts – likely via a cost advantage – since it offers less potential economic reward.

Consider the cord-cutting example from Chapter 1. The main benefit of cord cutting is that you get to watch the shows you want to watch, when you want to watch them. When compared with the need to conform to someone else's predetermined schedule, it is unequivocally better to have the flexibility to watch your show on your time. Even if by some amazing coincidence you wanted to watch the shows at the exact time that all the networks scheduled them, you would be no worse off than before. In this case, there is no uncertainty around the trend's desirability. Cord cutting is clearly better for consumers, so the question is whether you can overcome the feasibility and viability barriers.

Naturally, desirability is always relative: defined by the perspective of any individual consumer. Each has different tastes and might find different things attractive. Therefore, you should never (only) look at the market on an aggregate basis. Even with cord cutters, where the feature of being able to watch your shows when you want is better for all, that feature may be of more or less importance to different segments of the population. Especially in the early stages of a trend's appearance, "superusers" who are more willing to break long-standing habits to adopt a new behavior hold the key to understanding what the future might have in store.

Consider the launch of ride-hailing services. In markets like New York, where the existing taxi infrastructure didn't allow for calling a taxi, or consumers didn't find the experience clean, having the ability to hail a clean car from your phone at a similar price is unequivocally more desirable for the vast majority of consumers (granted a small minority just *liked* the yellow cab experience or took some comfort in the fact they were regulated). All the existing features are present with zero trade-off. However, other segments of the market might include significant trade-offs. In London, for instance, where taxi drivers are required to go through comprehensive training, there might be a trade-off on knowledgeability of the driver.[5] Or in other markets where it was easy to phone for a taxi, the trade-off might have been less obvious. Therefore, it was quite predictable that ride hailing would take off quicker in markets with less attractive existing competition (other things being equal). The question was not "if" but "when."

At this point, some readers may be wondering – "Wait, don't these if-to-when rollercoasters come in different sizes and shapes?" Absolutely: slopes vary, the height of the peaks vary, and the overall cycle time passing through the phase change from "if" to "when" varies as well. This additional dimension of "to what extent" a trend matters naturally leads to the question of how to know which early, weak signals to pay attention to. There is sadly no simple answer to this. The best provocateurs pay attention to *all* weak signals, at least to begin with. As a general rule of thumb, anything that has the possibility of impacting your foundational business model – or mission – should be paid particular attention to. For our Al Bundy executive, his business model was predicated on bundling multiple products to derive higher revenue from a stable customer base. Early on, he should have recognized that having that 1.75% segment – with customer buying behavior signaling desire for unbundling and less traditional product features – grow substantially could disrupt his whole growth system. The trick is to develop a method to pay keen attention to all early and/or weak signals and quickly assess their possible level of influence on your model for success. There will be some red herrings in the mix, for sure, but better in the early stages to set the aperture purposefully wide rather than to apply inadvertent blinders.

Many trends are complicated to consider because they aren't easily characterized by unequivocal desirability. Typically, a feature will be desirable for some but not others. Consider the market for e-readers. There were many predictions that e-readers would eventually dominate the market since their inception in the late 1990s. However, as of a few years ago, they only accounted for about 20% of all U.S. book sales according to the Association of American Publishers. Penetration outside of the United States is lower, with user penetration in Europe approximately 12.5% in 2021 according to Statista. As it turns out, the segment of customers who only consume content digitally is small – about 7% of U.S. adults according to Pew research.[6] We might surmise that this segment might value portability, the ease to carry multiple books without adding weight, or values a lightweight reader (when compared to a new hardcover novel). Beyond weight, perhaps this segment might value searching, or carrying their entire library with them on the road. Our friend and colleague Maeghan Sulham (without whom this book wouldn't exist) reports that her family loves e-readers because they allow for reading in bed with the light off, meaning bed partners can sleep more easily.

Although there may be lots of benefits, this segment remains small, especially when compared to the 37% of readers, who according to Pew, read print books *only*. These consumers clearly don't care about weight, having a digital, searchable library, or reading with the lights out. Or if they do, they don't sufficiently care to change existing reading habits. Perhaps there are benefits only available in print books that they value above others – like the "feel," or the ability to have a book signed by an author. This sort of desirability pattern is far more common, with opportunities being relevant to some consumers, but not others.

As markets mature, new entrants find ways to address desirability gaps in smaller and smaller proportions of the population – a typical industry evolution. The initial entrant effectively "creates" the industry with the advent of a new product or service that defines the market (and since they are the only competitor, they are the "average" as well). Then other competitors enter with slightly different features – a higher quality version for a higher price, or a lower quality version for a lower price. Over time, the market fragments with different offers to satisfy the various stages of the market until it is no longer economically feasible to serve these different segments. Typically, this is when we start to see consolidation. We are increasingly seeing this process of innovation, fragmentation, and consolidation happening faster and faster as consumer adoption through widely used channels, like mobile apps, can take place quickly.

In the food delivery space, we initially saw several different players in various markets around the world. In the United States, it started with GrubHub, SeamlessWeb (which became

Seamless), and even the now "retro" MenuPages. Looking to capitalize on a growing market, we saw the entry of DoorDash, UberEats, Postmates, Caviar, and others. In Europe we had Takeaway.com based in the Netherlands and Just Eat in the UK, along with a variety of other services. Over time, this intensifying of competition has led to decreasing margins and more consumer choice. The decreasing margins in turn led to consolidation to find economies of scale. We have seen this over the last several years with the merger of Just Eat and Takeaway in Europe, which later purchased GrubHub (which had previously purchased Seamless). In late 2020, UberEats completed a multibillion-dollar deal to acquire Postmates. And DoorDash acquired Caviar, a service that specialized in upscale urban-area restaurants that do not typically deliver. A very fast consolidation indeed!

In *Provoke* we are going to focus primarily on the kinds of trends that define or redefine industries and secondarily on the trends that segment industries. Why? By definition, the trends that define or redefine industries are the trends with the biggest opportunity to improve lives for customers and society.

If *desirability* frames the potential opportunity, *feasibility* and *viability* are the governors of how fast it can happen. You may be able to identify many opportunities to improve the status quo, but you have to be able to bring them to fruition economically. Several barriers can stand between something that is clearly desirable but not ready for mainstream adoption. There are several categories of these barriers.

Behavioral feasibility sits at the intersection of desirability and feasibility. Probably the most important question of feasibility is whether or not customer behavior can be changed to accommodate the trend being evaluated. It's not enough to have a superior product or experience; that doesn't always win the day. Trying something new often involves breaking longstanding habits – some of the most powerful forces in the world of customer behavior. For example, while organizations have become more comfortable with the concept of remote working, it's not clear if the trend will accelerate or if employees will want to forgo their commutes entirely.

Forming a new habit is easier when it's forced upon you by strong external circumstances like a pandemic. It's an entirely different thing to create a new habit when there are no forces acting in your favor. As a result, it takes real momentum to accomplish the goal of crossing the important inflection point of behavioral feasibility. Customers have to become aware of the trend, try it, repeat it, and often share the experience with others in some meaningful way for consumer feasibility barriers to be overcome.[7] And by the way, we know some of you reading now are saying, "Does this really apply to my business, which is B2B?" The answer is 100% yes. You too have human beings making decisions about which products and services they buy, whom they get to bid on those services, and the organizational habits (or systems and processes) that they encourage regarding how they purchase from vendors.

Technical feasibility refers to the degree to which it is physically possible to do the things necessary to create the trend. For instance, Uber broke prior technical feasibility barriers by putting together their code with previously existing navigation capabilities. We know that self-driving cars are technically feasible. And the pandemic response showed that rapid vaccine development is also technically feasible, if other barriers can be lifted.

Regulatory feasibility answers the question of whether it's legal to create the trend. Regulations tend to be reactive to the market rather than proactive. To create a new market, you often must overcome existing regulatory barriers. Uber, for instance, challenged existing regulations around the world.

Another example is how SpaceX is engaging with the Indian Telecom Regulatory Authority (TRAI), to help solve an important challenge – high-speed Internet access across India. It is looking to launch a constellation of satellites in lower orbit capable of providing 150Mbps service where the average speed for the country is around 12Mbps. The project is meant to overcome outdated regulations which were designed for different services to solve an important access issue.[8] *Viability* asks whether it's *profitable* to create the trend. The answer to this question is almost always murky. There are rarely any economic guarantees. What matters most is whether someone sees a sufficiently (to them) clear path to make money in the future to bet on taking the necessary steps to bring the trend to fruition. This is by definition a subjective question; two different organizations might look at the same opportunity and draw very different conclusions. But the viability test only requires one to take the bet. To some extent, it doesn't matter whether the venture is truly profitable in the long run because market creation may happen in advance of profitability (again, see Uber). True economic viability can only be determined in hindsight.

So what happened to the market for bidets in the United States? Did it continue to surge over the "if-to-when" phase change, or did it fail to create enough momentum? The latter. Bidets had some interesting short-term spikes in sales, but the spike did not turn into a long-lasting trend toward installing bidets in U.S. homes. Our hypothesis is that, while those who have tried bidets in the past may well be passionate about their superior cleaning experience, an insufficient number of Americans have seen a bidet, let alone tried one. The TP shortage didn't last long enough to get into true required behavior adaptation; it was only a concern about a potential future shortage. Therefore, people responded by hunting down every spare toilet paper roll they could find. The brief spike in bidet buying is more likely than not the result of people who had previously been on the fence now taking the "plunge" and using this push to get off the sidelines.

We similarly saw a spike in the trial of wet toilet paper usage, a market that has been unable to meaningfully grow beyond the niche group who swear by its use. In Steve's household, wet toilet paper was a short-term substitute. The Goldbach household was more than happy to see the Dude Wipes run out and the Charmin return.

While some may say hindsight is 20/20, we believe that understanding patterns of how humans behave and industries evolve is critical to forming hypotheses that should drive organizations to DO SOMETHING! earlier than they would otherwise. The trouble is that because of many "fatal flaws," individuals and organizations fail to get to the starting line of forming these hypotheses about the future. In Chapter 3, we'll examine some of these human and organizational traits that create a narrowing of organizational peripheral vision leading to systematic blindness to emerging trends.

CHAPTER 3

Personal Patterns

Some of the stories that we use to bring concepts to life are fun to write: they're evocative, pleasant to remember, and the better ones are strangely apt. Others feel a bit cringe-worthy . . . because they are so archetypical as to sound ripped from the reels of a corporate training video. Here's the thing, though: not only is this story real, but versions of this story happen all the time to the two of us. We've sat through meetings countless times – and we're sure you have, too – where it's going well until someone makes a comment from which a pile-on ensues.

With that, let's play the training video . . .

"I thought we were finally going to move! But in the end, we acted like ourselves again. Can I ask a favor? Can we chat for a minute tomorrow, early your time?"

Geoff looked down at his phone at the text from an old client in the United Kingdom. He had worked with Sammy for a long time at his prior company, but they hadn't spoken for a while as Sammy adjusted to his new company and role. Geoff was curious to hear what was going on when the phone rang the following morning.

After pleasantries, Sammy jumped into what he wanted to share. "So, we have been working on this new product launch for the last several months. I'm really excited, and so is the vast majority of the management team when we talk about things in private. But get them into a meeting, and all of a sudden the enthusiasm at the water cooler turns into silence in the meeting."

Geoff asked Sammy to share an example of a recent meeting. "We had come into this session with some new thinking to share. We showed that there is a group of customers that should be highly likely to adopt a new offer we've been toying around with. We've learned a lot about the needs of this group and feel like they will be very willing to pay for this "concierge" level of service. I've been trying to get the team to let us launch a prototype at a few stores in some key markets just to try it out. But every meeting is kind of like *Groundhog Day*."

"Say more," said Geoff.

Sammy continued, "So I was in the meeting, and we presented the analysis, mostly to head nods. Not a lot of negative comments throughout. There were five people in the meeting with me. One of them – Joe – spoke first as we moved out of the presentation into discussion: 'I'm supportive. I really think the concierge program is a big opportunity and we need to move on it quickly.' Then, Reshmi shared a similar perspective: 'I like it, too. I also don't think the competition is looking at anything similar so we can get out ahead.' Two other people nodded.

"I then said, 'Okay, great. I'll get the team moving on a prototype.' I thought we were moving forward this time. I really did. Then the fifth person, Molly, who had been sitting silently said, 'One quick question, Sammy. Have you guys given any thought to how we'll scale this across some of the smaller markets? I know we're starting in the large markets, which makes a ton of sense. Have we thought about how we'll roll this out to the broader markets?'"

Geoff knew what was coming next.

Sammy continued. "'Actually, Molly, given the proportion of our sales that come from smaller markets, we haven't given this a ton of thought. We think that if we are successful in large markets, that's a win in and by itself.'"

Sammy sighed. "That's when the floodgates opened. Antonio then weighed in. 'Molly makes a good point. It's probably not a bad idea to put some thinking behind this.' And then came Paula. 'I agree, it can't hurt.' Joe then sealed the deal. 'Sammy, why don't we give you a few weeks to think this through, and then we can see your analysis.'"

It was at this point that Sammy picked up the phone and called Geoff. He was at his wits' end and ready to quit.

"Honestly: we have to make a move here or we'll be stuck trying to play catch-up. Why is it that herd mentality tends to favor caution and incrementalism instead of being bold?!"

We expect that the story depicted in the "training video" is recognizable to most of you. It happens just about every day in organizations around the world. A combination of basic human biases – what we call fatal flaws – and organizational dysfunction mean that most businesses systematically miss the opportunity to take early action against emerging trends – whether they are still in the "if" stage or the early stages of "when." They wait until the only choice is one of adaptation.

We call these cognitive biases "fatal flaws" only somewhat in jest. People aren't literally dying from them, but they can make the difference between an organization failing or thriving. Successfully spotting subtle – or not-so-subtle – trends that meaningfully impact the prospects for businesses is a fundamentally important capability that impacts every business, big or small, old economy or new economy, virtual or physical.

When businesses are faced with fundamental changes to the environment in which they operate, leaders have a choice – *but only if they can effectively identify the meaningful trends*. Those choices involve either riding the trend downwards, adjusting the business model to fit the emerging trend, or shaping the trend to create advantage. None of these is a "wrong" choice, by the way. Riding a trend downwards can be a very profitable choice. Many diversified companies that had tobacco divisions have spun them into singular entities that have no other businesses, and they pay massive dividends, despite having an addressable market that shrinks every year. The problem is, most companies that end up in wind-down mode do so accidentally ... missing any opportunity to create advantage along the way.

Choosing not to adjust your business model means the company is effectively choosing to be a wind-down firm – one that has a finite life, a business that is terminal. They're winding

down, even if executives in the industry fail to recognize this fact. Print publishing companies that choose not to migrate to a digital platform in the face of shrinking paper readership or traditional department stores that do not adjust their core value proposition (i.e., everything under one roof) in the face of intense online competition are examples of this. The question that will most likely impact the amount of value created during the wind-down is whether the move is executed as a purposeful choice, or inadvertently because all other options have dried up.

At the end of *Detonate* we pondered the value of being a pop-up firm: one that is formed and launched with a planned extinction date. Temporary retail stores – ones for limited edition goods in Japan or Halloween costumes in the United States – are great examples of this. Vaccine sites (we hope, at the time of writing) could be another. These entities have taken the ultimate step in embracing impermanence as a way to create advantage for themselves. Bringing some of the pop-up mindset to the wind-down world, whether you end up there with foresight or by accident, is a critical tool for any company operating in an uncertain market. Based on our experience, though, we think most management teams want to avoid being wind-down firms. Unfortunately, they don't make the logic clear with the other members of the management team. We believe that having an *explicit conversation* about whether to ride a falling trend or make the necessary investment to evolve a business model is critical – and most organizations never have this conversation as a result of the fatal flaws.

There's nothing fundamentally wrong with either strategic path. Winding down a company over a period of time can be very profitable. And adaptation can be really hard. However, one recipe for failure is to try to operate as if you're going to last forever when the external conditions dictate winding down. Here's the crux of the reason that cognitive biases and organizational dysfunction are so detrimental. Many management teams don't identify the trends, they don't have the conversation, and then they fall into predictable patterns that avoid putting critical issues on the table to decide whether to adapt to the emerging trend or wind down the company.

The first step in adapting is seeing change in the external environment, and the second is choosing to respond. If you can't even see the changes coming, you can't get to a point where you can effectively debate how you'll respond and, even at that point, other biases prevent action. Companies must be aware of the human biases that create the precondition for systematic organizational blindness and inaction. Let's explore several of the cognitive biases, starting with those that make it hard to see trends.

Availability bias. If we had a nickel for every time someone, when challenging market research, cited preference of a family member to discredit or support the research, we'd have a lot of nickels. You've probably been in a meeting like this, too, where someone would say something like, "I gave a sample to my daughter and she hated it." Although it's unfortunate that his daughter disliked the product, it certainly does not imply that the research is faulty. It's also clear that, in addition to not appreciating the relevance of sampling size, the person in question might be suffering from the availability bias – that is, the tendency to rely on examples that are easy to access mentally. It was challenging for our friend in Chapter 1 to see the possibility of cord cutting because the concept simply wasn't mentally accessible to him at that point.

We would be remiss if we didn't note that the availability bias is certainly contributing to the current divided state of American politics. Social media has become an echo chamber and we are no longer exposed to other ideas or concepts and, as a result, find other points of view "wacky" or disproportionately "out of step." It's too easy not to stretch to find new information or to try to adopt a different point of view when information that supports your preconceptions is so readily available.

Egocentric bias. Whereas the availability bias is about what information is more proximate to an individual, the egocentric bias is the tendency to overweight data that is consistent with one's previous point of view. Why is this important? The world is a muddy place and there is often lots of data that is unclear. If you are more likely to select and use data that conforms to your view of the world, then it makes it harder for you to incorporate different views into your overall perspective. Interestingly, there is data that shows that people who are bilingual are less subject to egocentric bias because they have grown up paying attention to others' points of view. When there are new trends that don't conform to your worldview, it's harder to see them – and even harder to incorporate them into your decision-making about how to respond. (The egocentric bias also tends to result in people overestimating their contributions to a group and underweighting the contributions of others, but, from the point of view of what causes people to *miss* trends, we are less interested in that aspect of the bias.[1])

The egocentric bias may have developed because the human brain is better at coding things into memory when individuals believe that information will have an impact on them. At some point in our evolutionary history, this may have had advantages to our survival. Now, it challenges our ability to succeed if humans are less able to incorporate data that is not obviously connected to our current worldview.

Affect heuristic bias. This bias suggests that people base their judgments on their perceived affect toward what they are judging. Here, *affect* refers to the size of the emotional response (either good or bad) associated with the stimulus. Essentially, affect heuristic is a "gut" response to something that is triggered when we have strong feelings associated with the subject.[2]

The reason affect heuristic is partially responsible for the systematic blindness of people toward new – or distant – trends is that small trends are unlikely to provoke any emotional response. In our example in Chapter 1, our executive was unconcerned about a 1.75% segment because it didn't trigger any emotional response because it was overwhelmingly small compared to his overall market share. We also see this in people who try to get healthy. For many, the immediate response to exercising is that it "hurts" (a strong negative emotion) but the potential health benefits (a strong positive emotion) don't happen for a long time.

Each of the preceding three biases contributes in part to the inability of individuals to see trends that are at the "if" stage, or even the early "when" stage. They may not be in the available array of data that leaders assess, or they are discounted because they don't conform to their views, or they don't elicit an emotional response because of how distant they are. Taken together, "if" issues tend not to get raised within an organization until they might trigger some emotional response in someone (usually labeled an alarmist within the organization). Although we can't say this definitively, our strong hypothesis is that by the time something is triggering an emotional reaction, it's highly likely that the trend is at the far end of the "when" stage, when options for influence are limited.

The challenge of not seeing trends is further exacerbated by the human tendencies that prevent action against those trends. Several well-known biases include:

Status quo bias. This is a pretty straightforward bias: a preference for the status quo over a change. One explanation for this bias is that a deviation from the status quo is perceived by people as "losing" something – and humans are quite loss averse. Another explanation is that the status quo requires less cognitive effort to comprehend and maintain, while thinking about change requires more effort.[3]

The status quo bias is key when applied to organizational challenges. In our experience, we see a pervasive behavior from management teams that is rooted in the status quo. Imagine a management team meeting to evaluate a new product for launch. They will rightly name all the risks associated with the move against the potential upside. In most cases, they *implicitly* compare it to a baseline characterized by the status quo. For instance, consider the following typical risks that one might hear in a management meeting:

> "It may not work as we anticipate, and our competition will gain share."
>
> "Our customers may not give us brand permission."
>
> "Our channels won't want to stock it."
>
> "There's no way sales will go for it."
>
> "The lawyers will just say 'no.'"

Of course, all of those are distinct possibilities, but the comparison is implicitly to a status quo that is riskless. Management teams almost never take the status quo and assess all the risks associated with *not* launching the product – risks such as *maybe our competitors will launch something faster* or *if we don't launch it and our competitors do, we will lose customers in the future.* The way human beings tend to think about the status quo naturally positions any deviation from it as a "loss." In other words, it makes the status quo a "stock" value (measured at one point in time – the present), rather than a "flow" value (measured over time).

Overconfidence bias. Another bias that makes action difficult is being overconfident in one's likelihood of being correct. People overestimate the likelihood that they are correctly judging a situation. They underestimate the chance that they are wrong. Several studies have demonstrated this bias by asking people to answer questions such as how to spell words or true/false statements on general knowledge topics, and then assessing their confidence in their answers. Systematically, people overestimate their chance of being correct. In other words, on questions they say they are 100% certain they are right, they are only correct say 90% of the time, and on questions they feel they are 80% right, they are correct less than 80% of the time.[4]

Combining these – when you couple the overconfidence bias with the availability heuristic, in which people don't see possibilities they are not intimately familiar with, and don't adequately assess the risks of the status quo – makes it easy to see how human beings are prone to systematic misevaluation of the potential impact of emerging trends that are not yet pervasive in their world. They just miss and/or dismiss them as a result of being typical human beings.

It would be great if organizational behaviors tended to correct for these human fallacies but, sadly, they don't. They do the opposite, reinforcing them and increasing the likelihood that humans fall prey to these tendencies. Several ways that human biases are reinforced in organizations include the following:

Embarrassment in meetings. How many meetings have you been in in which you had something important to say that disagreed with the consensus but you held your tongue just in case you were wrong? Or how many times did a disagreement start to develop when someone interjected to suggest "taking it offline"? Taking it offline is the widespread phenomenon that supposedly "saves" people from having to discuss challenging topics in groups. A successful meeting is one in which everyone agreed and people left feeling good – or the boss is happy. One of our very close friends was once brought to a meeting as a summer intern to keep the boss from yelling, because the team surmised that the boss wouldn't yell in the presence of an intern.

We look at meetings as something to get through while keeping face rather than a setting to discuss and debate important topics. This is corporate theater and not real discussion. Everything is prewired and socialized so that nobody has to disagree in the presence of others. Frankly, the two of us wish we might have lived in the time of Alfred Sloan, who once famously said, "I propose we postpone further discussion of this matter until our next meeting to give ourselves time to develop disagreement and perhaps gain understanding of what the decision is all about."

If management teams are literally unable to create meeting space where legitimate disagreements are raised, not only because people might be embarrassed but because successful meetings are characterized as the kind where people *don't* disagree, then they will increasingly be unable to see and debate emerging threats.

Fear of embarrassment is a form of loss aversion on an organizational scale. People don't want to be seen to be wrong in meetings because organizational culture tends to deem being wrong as a loss of status.

Cognitive bandwidth of leadership. There is a demonstrated bias in psychology called the *scarcity effect* that makes people value things that are scarce above things that are plentiful. It used to be that only the very most senior executive leadership had their calendars characterized by wall-to-wall meetings. Now it's everyone in the organization. Our hypothesis is that the number of meetings is inversely correlated with the challenges of scheduling them. Prior to pervasive calendar software, one might see a handful of meetings per day. Now that we can simply go onto someone's calendar and see their open time, plop, there is another meeting. As a result, people have less time to do actual work and think. Some calendaring software now provides for the ability to recapture "focusing time," because the need for scheduling time to think is greater than ever.[5]

What does this mean in practice and what does it have to do with the ability to see trends? Time has become the scarce resource. The two of us, if bored in meetings, usually like to try to make a game of estimating when someone will inevitably say "in the interest of time" (as if time were a stakeholder that needed representation in the meeting). We each try to call the precise time when it will be said (for example, 6 minutes to go, 3 minutes to go). Time spent in discussion and debate is cut short because there's another meeting to go to. We almost never hear someone say, "This is a really important topic and I know we all have other meetings, but let's spend more time on this." Discussions are snuffed out.

This is particularly problematic for our most senior leaders. Their days are filled with meetings, travel, and meals with not a lot of time for themselves or to think. As Michael Porter and Nitin Nohria wrote in *Harvard Business Review*, "CEOs are always on, and there is always more to be done. The leaders in our study worked 9.7 hours per weekday, on average. They also conducted business on 79% of weekend days, putting in an average of 3.9 hours daily, and on 70% of vacation days, averaging 2.4 hours daily. As these figures show, the CEO's job is relentless."[6] As a result, they rarely have sufficient time to think about the future and the challenges their businesses might face in the future. Too many organizations are governed by the tyranny of the urgent.

Escalation of commitment tendencies. Perhaps the ultimate expression of the status quo bias is the tendency to increase the level of commitment to a choice despite increasingly negative outcomes. The classic business example of this is the now infamous choice by Blockbuster Video to declare that it was in the "store" business versus the DVD-to-home business, even in the face of increasing evidence that customers preferred the emerging model of DVD-to-home. An even more costly escalation of commitment can happen in military conflicts; once military action is taken, it is difficult to de-escalate until one side is defeated.

Organizational politeness and desire for full consensus. Another organizational tendency is that people can be overly polite in groups, not willing to have "sharp elbows" or embarrass anyone during meetings. This is perhaps the flipside of the don't-be-embarrassed phenomenon. But there are in fact bad ideas.

There are also ideas that, although not bad per se, are knowingly impractical. However, we observe that rather than be honest with the person about why the idea is bad or why it is impractical, the group suggests that it can be investigated further to be polite. This has the unintended consequence of delaying action on the critical path and wasting resources on ideas that are not fundamentally valuable.

Naturally, this begs the question: How can you tell the difference between a bad idea and important, well-intentioned dissent, a critical feature of great management decisions and innovation? And how do you make sure people feel empowered to raise ideas that might be a source of important correction or inspiration?

We'll examine this further in Chapter 4, but it's critical to understand the underlying rationale for the perspective, not just its existence. Our preferred method of addressing this challenge (which is far superior to avoiding conflict by "taking it offline" or agreeing to do more work unnecessarily) is to play a game of HBD . . . and we don't mean Happy Birthday. *HBD* stands for *hunch*, *bias*, or *data*. Lest we cause some confusion, in this game, the meaning of bias does not refer to the cognitive kind, but rather a personal tendency (e.g., Geoff's bias is to get stuff off his plate and never touch it again; Steve's bias is to talk things through . . . and through).

In this game, you ask the person floating the idea to share their logic and whether their idea is a hunch, a bias, or based on data. If it's a bias (for instance, they just prefer to study things more) or a hunch without compelling logic ("It just feels that way to me"), then it's fair to let the group know that, given a broad consensus otherwise, the group should move forward. But if the logic is compelling and based on real observations or data, then the group should give it stronger consideration. Although perhaps not a perfect antidote, this should help solve the difficult challenge of wanting to invite dissent, especially from diverse voices who may not feel as comfortable speaking up without compelling the group to run down every idea. Over time, groups must demonstrate that they value ideas with terrific logic.

Structural dismantling of organizational curiosity. Our final fatal flaw is the tendency by many organizations to underfund – or completely cut – exploratory learning budgets when push comes to shove. It happens so frequently it's almost cliche: at the start of budget season, everyone says it's important to go and learn about customers and their environments . . . but by the end of the season, someone points out that this spending can't directly tie to revenue next year, so it gets eliminated. No leader would say they aren't curious about the customers and markets they serve, but most organizations behave as if they aren't. You can't claim curiosity that you don't follow through on. And if you aren't actively looking, you won't see the new and important trends on the horizon in time to DO SOMETHING valuable about them.

When all of this is taken together, what do we end up with? We have people in organizations who are biased against even seeing possible impactful trends in the marketplace, just by the nature of being human – not because they are incompetent or evil. If they do identify a trend, they are biased against seeing it as important to their business and tend to discount it entirely. And if a trend does get raised, there are considerable organizational impediments to taking any meaningful action against it.

In other words, the dynamic interaction of human tendencies with organizational dysfunction produces systematic blindness that decreases the potential playing field for organizations. Failure to see possibilities makes it increasingly likely that organizations end up pursuing an implicit "wind-down firm" strategy on a slope to irrelevancy, following a shrinking market to its very bottom.

But we think there are ways for companies to pursue strategies that have them adapt and thrive. We'll explore some basic tactics for how to address systemic individual blindness in the next chapter before turning our attention to more advanced provocation strategies in Part II.

CHAPTER 4

Expanding Peripheral Vision

"I can't deal with this anymore! I'm done. I'm walking over to HR and asking them to give me a package!"

William was exasperated and frustrated. He was one of the most senior and accomplished men at his consumer products company. But he had a new boss who was completely different from his prior boss. William and Steve were debriefing in the cafeteria after the latest interaction with the new boss. Steve hadn't seen William like this in the years they had worked together. It was taking its toll on him. He had become short with others and was frequently and visibly frustrated. It was notably out of character.

William was usually incredibly confident in his manner with others – not cocky, but supremely capable. When he met with others, he deftly controlled the direction of the conversation. He listened to others but always drove to the outcome he had been planning. He entered each meeting with a clear objective on what he sought to accomplish with the other person (particularly when it was a senior person) and almost always achieved it.

His experience with his new boss, Beth, was different. He had had a series of challenging conversations with her from which he walked away feeling frustrated. Steve had been involved in a number of these and it wasn't that the conversations had been uncomfortable or delicate. But they did seem to be going in a lot of different directions.

"I don't get it, Steve. We walk in with exactly what she asked for previously and then it's like we're in the Twilight Zone. It seems like in the last two weeks, everything she had asked for has somehow changed. I know people always said Beth was LIFO" (this was a joke someone in the organization had made up about senior executives who repeat what they heard in recent meetings – the last in their office was the first thing that came out of their mouth), "but this back and forth is killing me. We aren't making progress."

Steve knew something had to change. It wasn't because William seemed upset at Beth. Actually, from Steve's perspective, Beth was highly engaged, calm, and expressed appreciation for William's work. But it was becoming increasingly apparent that William was getting impatient with Beth, and it was starting to leak into meetings. He was more apt to – not so subtly – remind Beth, "We've given that to you a few meetings back – *remember*? Or to tell her that her ideas probably wouldn't work: "We thought of that, too, but discarded it because . . ." Beth generally listened but was undeterred by William's more frequent objections. She would smile and say things like, "Let's just take a look at it this way once. Humor me."

They were indeed going around in circles. William felt Beth was squishy, and Beth was experiencing William as linear. Something had to change. We suggested that William seek some counsel from someone who knew both of them and was trained in "productive interactions."

The person who knew them both, Deepti, talked to each of them individually about what they wanted to accomplish in their interactions. As it turned out, Beth was not in a bad place at all. She thought the conversations were fine – although she did see William getting increasingly frustrated at something and didn't want to call it out. Deepti made an interesting insight about how they behaved in meetings based on her experience and training. We aren't going to go into detail here (there are lots of instruments to compare operating preferences), but Deepti was trained to look for the implicit "rules" you follow when interacting with others.

Deepti intuited that William preferred "closed" interactions. In closed interactions, the person with authority for the conversation drives the interaction. Importantly, it's not about position in the organization but rather authority in the conversation and, since William was bringing the information, he thought he should be in the driver's seat. But then, since he had this "closed" tendency, when Beth would say what she wanted him to do next, he would just do it.[1]

Beth, on the other hand, was more "random," a preference for a conversation with a lack of official structure. Whoever needs the authority in the moment should seize it, and newness and novelty are encouraged. Random should not be confused with an "open" preference, which is structured to allow participation from everyone in an organized way.

Neither of these are inherently good or bad. People who have a random profile, like Beth, tend to be good in situations where creativity is necessary for problem solving, and those who are more closed tend to be better when follow-through is key. The issue, though, was that the interaction between these ways of operating – between William and Beth – was creating a precondition for an increasingly unproductive relationship. As it turned out, Beth was happy because what she wanted to do was explore issues and she just did that. She wasn't deciding anything in the meeting; she was exploring.

But William took Beth's musings to mean *this is what I want*, based on his tendencies and on the expectations of those people he had worked with previously. So William left meetings thinking he had clear marching orders for action before the next meeting. Beth left the meeting thinking they had an interesting conversation that she wanted William to reflect on a bit more before their next conversation when they would continue to explore the issue until they reached a resolution.

The problem was that their profiles were invisible to each other. When Deepti talked to the two of them together, she gave them explicit instructions to share more of what they wanted to accomplish with each other. She told Beth to be clearer when she was in "explore" mode and told William to check with Beth on whether he should take her comments as decisions or just "thinking out loud." Just naming the differences in their approach allowed Beth and William to approach the meetings differently because they now had some visibility into what the other might be thinking and experiencing.

Before the intervention, neither Beth, nor William, nor their organization was getting the benefit of their different approaches. Rather, it was causing stagnation. The fatal flaws were getting in the way. Deepti's intervention also shows us a way forward by creating some visibility so that the fatal flaws can be proactively addressed.

In this chapter we'll explore some relatively straightforward (but not easy) ways that companies can start to address these flaws today. These are tactics you can adopt that will expand your, and your organization's peripheral vision so that you can see more of the playing field, and so you'll be more likely to see the "if-to-when" trends and more prepared to take on our Provoke strategies.

EMBRACE DIVERSITY

One of the best antidotes to a narrowing of organizational peripheral vision is to embrace diversity. Said simply, more diverse groups are better at solving complex problems and creating new possibilities. Let's unpack that further.

In his body of work on productive interactions, the late Harvard professor Chris Argyris created a metaphor called the "ladder of inference." The concept came with one of the odder clip-art creations that we've seen: a ladder in a pool. The pool was meant to represent the pool of information or data that was available to any individual. Argyris shared that individuals, in reaching conclusions, select some data from the available pool and then interpret the data using their own models of the world, which are based on their learned heuristics and experiences.

One of the most powerful things that Argyris surmised was that people frequently speak to each other at the level of a *conclusion* rather than sharing the data or how they interpreted the data. As a result, when people disagree, they may be doing so simply because they aren't looking at the foundational information that drew them to different conclusions. Argyris would say that more productive interactions start with using inquiry to draw out other people's ladders so that, if there are differences in data (not hunches or biases) about the world, their differences can be compared and tested. These interactions are more productive because they advance understanding about the other person, and the world, by exploring what data each individual brings to the conversations and their model of the world.

The important point here is that the two interests involved have to see the world differently, a concept called "cognitive diversity." Over the years, there have been many studies on the benefits of cognitive diversity as it relates to problem solving and prediction. Throughout this chapter, we will draw heavily on the work of Scott Page, a professor at the University of Michigan. Scott was kind enough to spend a few hours with us discussing his work. We will also draw upon his collaborations with Katherine Phillips, a professor at Northwestern University (who sadly passed away all too early in January 2020), and Sheen Levine, a professor at the University of Texas at Dallas. At its foundation, their work, collectively, has shown – "mathematically," as Page put it when we talked with him – that more diverse groups are better at solving problems.[2]

A good analogy for the impact of diversity on problem solving is diversification in investment portfolios. Investing in a diversified portfolio rather than just a few individual securities allows investors to meaningfully reduce risk while keeping expected returns about the same – effectively a "bonus" from diversification: the bonus being reduced risk. Stocks go up and down for many reasons, but broadly their ups and downs can be bucketed into two categories: market risk and company-specific risk. Ice cream companies all suffer from the same market risk: really cold summers lead to low demand for ice cream, for example. A company-specific risk might involve labor relations that threaten supply during a sweltering summer when everyone else is thriving.

When you have many securities in a portfolio, you tend to diversify away the company-specific risk. Some companies will have bad luck such as a strike at the ice cream plant, but others might discover the hot new flavor that takes off. And because you can invest in both umbrella and ice cream companies, you can hedge the risk of bad summer weather. Therefore, in a diversified portfolio, you tend to get the same average return *but with lower risk* – the bonus.

The same idea applies to groups solving complex problems. If you diversify the group working on a problem, you'll more likely get the right answer. How does this work mathematically? Scott Page explains it using the following formula:

Group Error = Average Individual Error – Diversity

During our Zoom meeting, Scott explained the benefit of diversity against problem solving using the simile of an episode of the television show *CSI*. After interviewing one witness, you have a single angle on the crime in question. You might be able to eliminate one or two suspects. But as you keep adding eyewitnesses, each of whom had a different angle on the crime, you can incrementally eliminate suspects and are more likely to find the perpetrator. But interviewing a bunch of eyewitnesses who saw the crime from the same angle advances the investigation less.

We challenged Scott about whether this works on knowable problems only, or if it worked when a group is trying to generate new possibilities. It turns out the answer is both – and it's an amazing benefit. Stuart Kauffman coined the term "adjacent possibilities" in the field of biology. During our conversation, we applied the concept to opportunity development. It turns out that not only does having a diverse group allow for more possibilities because everyone brings a different point of view, but those different points of view open up adjacent ideas latent in the group that wouldn't have come up without the benefit of the diversity.

Scott shared the following example. A company is thinking about where to place their next manufacturing plant. Two folks in the group are debating – Peoria or Springfield. Someone walks in on the conversation and says, "How about Berlin?" All of a sudden, this new framing of the problem expands the frames of the first two participants. They hadn't thought about possibilities outside the United States. One participant, whose family is from Germany, notes that actually Hamburg would be a terrific idea to consider. And that opens up another possibility for the third person, who now realizes that on their last trip to Europe, they heard something about government incentives for manufacturing coming out of Poland, so Warsaw gets added to the list of possibilities. The single adjacent possibility created a cascade of further adjacent possibilities.

Leveraging Argyris's language and a nonmathematical, logical approach, groups benefit from cognitive diversity because each individual in the group selects different data based on their personal biases, processes that data differently based on their experiences and learned heuristics, and reaches different conclusions. As long as the group interacts productively (that is, they listen to one another and draw out the important differences), by the nature of their interaction, the group should "see" more data and process it in multiple ways that are much more likely to get to the "correct" answer – or answers.

Here's how cognitive diversity ties into the kind of diversity that organizations are often concerned about – identity diversity. While cognitive diversity refers to differences in how people process problems, those personal heuristics are a product of the collective set of experiences that a person has – where they grew up, what they've been taught, how they've lived, what they've seen, and how they've felt throughout these experiences. All of those things are heavily influenced by classic measures of diversity – skin color/race, ethnicity, gender, country/city of origin, sexual orientation, religion, socioeconomic status, and so on. All these things cause people to select and process data differently, resulting in different ways each individual might tackle a problem. That is, classic measures of diversity are likely to lead to cognitive diversity.

We want to be clear that we support diversity not just because it's efficacious in making decisions. Diversity, equity, and inclusion all have deeply moral dimensions that are just as important as, if not more important than solutions of any immediate business problem at hand.

So, diversity in and by itself is a clear way to directly address the fatal flaws that narrow organizational peripheral vision. But that can't be addressed overnight. There are, however, things that organizations can do to take advantage of diversity they already have.

Teach productive interactions to embrace inclusion. Unfortunately, in many organizations minorities and women don't feel as empowered to speak up and speak their minds as their white male counterparts. As a result, organizations do not get the benefits of the diversity they have already. Why? Getting the benefit of diversity means that the data they select and their data processing mechanisms have to be included in the way the problem is solved. If these groups feel less willing to speak their minds, then the group doesn't get the benefit of their perspectives. To overcome this, Argyris's teaching trains people to pair *advocacy* with *inquiry*. The goal is to make sure that each member of the group is willing to *advocate* for the things they see, sharing the data and the logic for how they reached their conclusions. But, importantly, they also *inquire* about the data and logic of others, with the intent to learn about the way others perceive the world. This is a learned skill and it takes a lifetime to perfect. A simple reminder before every meeting goes a long way. You can say to yourself, "I have a point of view worth hearing, but I might be missing something." Acting consistently with the teachings of productive interaction is a great way to promote inclusion.

Don't just staff the experts. As we've noted in previous writings, a "beginners mind" is a powerful tool. Organizations tend to call in the experts when they want something done "right," whether it's the finance team leading the budget exercise, HR leading evaluation systems, or the strategy team creating the company's direction. As it turns out, teams comprised of only subject-matter experts can underperform teams comprised of traditional experts mixed with skills from other functions. The same logic we've been applying holds in this situation as well. The incremental benefit from adding another "expert" is low because they tend to have similar heuristics and models of problem solving and tend to select the same data as one another. A person with a different set of heuristics is likely to provide different inputs that improve the outcome. Scott Page has shown that you can actually create better economic forecasts by including a mix of economists and other experts on teams. This kind of diversity should apply to other problems as well, so as companies have important, complex tasks, make sure they are staffed by multifunctional teams.

Avoid activities that reinforce the "siren call of sameness," a term coined by Sheen Levine. Let's face it: as human beings, our tendency is to look for the things that we all have in common. When we meet new people, smalltalk is usually centered on things like figuring out if we went to the same school, play the same sport, or know the same people. There is a natural desire for connection, especially with people we want to like, and liking often begins with commonalities.

Unfortunately, this tendency has consequences. Think, for instance, about the standard process for getting a job. First, you might need to "network" to get to available job opportunities. People are more likely to pass you on based on something in common (i.e., we went to the same school); for evidence, look no further than the implicit value proposition when top schools talk about their alumni network for proof of that. Then, once you've got a pile of resumes, the candidates get interviewed. Candidates who succeed in standard interview processes are the ones who are able to make connections . . . again, based disproportionately on what people have in common. As a consequence, the kinds of activities organizations typically use to create our teams actually work against our having diverse teams.

This is an issue that all organizations should and can address. Some organizations are already making progress. Many are moving away from the standard conversational interview as the centerpiece of the evaluation process. Google, for example, has its candidates take online assessments and complete project work prior to getting jobs. And if you must interview, it's a "must" to provide protocols to prevent your people (typically your senior people, who will *insist* they know how to interview someone based on the years they have done it) from "winging it."[3]

Make "flexibility in thinking" a positive leadership trait. The term *flip-flopping* will cause many of us of a certain age to think back to the 2004 presidential race between George W. Bush and John Kerry. One of the claims of the Bush campaign was that Kerry had changed his position over the years on many different issues. They charged that he initially supported the war in Vietnam and then subsequently was against it, for instance. They were positioning this as a poor quality of leadership; good leaders, they implied, were steadfast and did not change their positions over time. They even handed out flip-flops at the convention to further cement the branding. One cannot know whether this really helped Bush to handily win reelection over Kerry in 2004, but it certainly is one of the most memorable parts of the campaign.

We must dispel the notion that strong leaders don't change their positions . . . or, dare we say, learn. We're not suggesting that flip-flopping with no explanation is a desired leadership trait: that amounts to just whipsawing the organization by constantly changing your tune about an issue with no basis for the change other than it's Tuesday and you felt bored and decided you believed something different. However, flip-flopping when you have new information – flexing your thinking in an explicable way – is absolutely a hallmark of effective leadership in the face of accelerating change.

Rather, we think that leadership needs to be in a constant state of recommitment to their ideals and beliefs. We pointed out in *Detonate* that strategies don't come with a predetermined expiration date; they aren't deli meat. But over time, they do tend to get stale. Good strategy-setting processes make clear the "critical conditions" that need to exist for the strategy to be successful. Roger Martin, our friend and colleague, coined the logical test of "what must be true" to ask about effective strategies. Good leaders have an intuitive sense of the things that must be true for their organization to be successful and consistently check whether these conditions remain true in the external environment. They are on the lookout for things that could destroy the business model they have created. And if something changes that gives them pause, they aren't afraid to make adjustments. When your business model may be at risk of implosion, it's a very good thing that leaders changed their tune.

Maintaining a course that is heading straight into trouble is like sailing with great confidence straight into the path of a giant iceberg – and we all know of at least one instance of how that turned out. Of course, it makes all the sense in the world to change course in the face of new and different data about a projected path. Good leaders shouldn't be compelled to stay the course because the captain must go down with the ship. We must learn to admire the fearless leader who has the courage to say, "Yes, I used to support a particular course of action, but in the wake of learning something new, I have changed my mind." That needs to be a good thing. Learning is cool. Failure is not.

Having said that, it's always important to share your rationale for the change. In his teaching on productive interactions, Argryis talked about the importance of not leaving those you were communicating with a lot of room to interpret your conclusions. Instead, he suggests you "walk down your ladder of inference" by sharing the data you're drawing from. Good leaders will constantly be on the lookout for those things that could change their outlook on a particular course of action. When they see something, they won't just shout "march left"; they will share the findings clearly and make others see what they are seeing.

Appoint a devil's advocate. One way that we can inject some dissent into groups intentionally is to appoint a "devil's advocate" in each meeting – especially those meetings where critical issues and decisions are being made. A devil's advocate is someone who intentionally argues for the opposite point of view in the spirit of injecting debate into a group where it

otherwise might not exist. The idea has its roots in the Catholic Church, which, in the sixteenth century, would appoint a church lawyer to argue against the canonization of a saint.

It seems pretty simple, but we know from experience that this happens rarely. And when it does, it's usually because there is actually a person with a different point of view in the room. That's a good thing, unless that person is always the "sticky wicket" because, over time, that person's point of view tends to be discounted by the group as "Tom just being Tom." Too often, the people with alternative perspectives don't speak up for fear of embarrassment. A good practice to counteract these tendencies is to appoint someone at the start of the meeting to formally play the role of the dissenter. You can't always count on Tom to speak up.

Appointing a devil's advocate should meet three important standards. First, you can't always appoint the same person. Ideally, the role would rotate, with everyone eventually taking part – from the most senior to the most junior. Having different voices is critical to the practice being effective. That way, nobody feels left out in participating in the exercise.

Second, it's important that the appointed devil's advocate takes it seriously and does not make comments like, "Well, I really don't believe this myself, but since I'm playing the devil's advocate, here's an alternative perspective." They have to play it as if they believe what they are saying – full stop. If someone can determine that they are not being real, then the practice will fail.

Third, the role has to be played in character for the duration or implied intent and meaning could get very confusing. Try to abolish the lead-in of "well, to play devil's advocate for a minute ..." On the surface, that may sound productive, but we find that more often than not that's really just a way of discounting all that is to follow. The undertone becomes one of

"Well, of course I don't actually believe this myself since I see it the way that all of you do . . . but let's pretend someone *had* to disagree."

Address implicit organizational incentives. Richard Thaler, a Nobel Prize–winning economist from the University of Chicago, created the idea of the "dumb principal problem" as a variant on the classic "principal–agent problem" to describe situations in which the people calling the shots create unintentional incentives that make it less likely to achieve the desired outcome. A common example of this is when managers are unwilling to take on "risky" projects, despite the potential for a meaningful upside, because of perceived risks to their career if they fail. Thaler calls it the "dumb principal" problem because it's the leader who sets up the management systems that promote this belief among the managers. (You might also call this the unintended consequences of bad incentives.) Management systems are probably the most important, yet most overlooked, aspects of creating a great strategy that works in practice. What are management systems? All the various organizational choices that drive the behavior of its people: culture, evaluation systems, budgets, organizational design, communication, among myriad other possibilities.

When Thaler talks about the "dumb principal," he's not talking (only) about situations in which an executive acts out of stupidity; it's also about situations in which the executive is clear-headed about a desired outcome and well-intentioned in setting up incentives to achieve it. The breakdown happens when that executive makes too many unspoken logical leaps from an incented behavior to the desired outcome. For example, if an innovation system is set up to incent the filling of the "front end" of a funnel – that is, quantity of early-stage ideas – under the presumption that more ideas means higher likelihood of in-market success, the "principal" who authorized that move would have been well-advised to consider its unintended consequences. What if we end up delaying time-to-market of one or two *great* ideas as the system gets locked up in sorting the inflow? Or what if organizational resources get redirected to focus on idea collection instead of idea commercialization? Or what if we fall prey to simple garbage-in/garbage-out? Leaders need to be master system designers to make sure they set up the right behavioral incentives to get the results consistent with their objectives.

Try anonymous meetings. If there is one thing the Internet has shown us, it's that people can be brutally honest if there is zero risk that they will be outed as themselves. While the world of Internet comments appears to vacillate between merely unseemly and downright abusive, we can learn something from how humans behave there.

On subjects that are particularly controversial, organizational leaders can use tools to create anonymity during meetings to foster a multiplicity of frank perspectives. The meetings need to be sufficiently large that it's unlikely that comments will be individually identifiable; 8 to 10 people seems to clear that hurdle based on our admittedly unscientific observations.

Why would this work? We just need to look back to the status quo bias of Chapter 3. If people are concerned that saying something controversial would make people think less of them, then creating anonymous meetings removes that risk. Now, they are free to actually provoke discussion without fear of repercussion. It also might be a way for leaders to inject provocation into the meeting. In using the technique ourselves, we've seen leaders use the anonymity tool to throw out some ideas that they might be thinking of that they've not wanted to insert into open conversations for fear that the organization will say "that's what that person *really* wants." Using this, on occasion, even to build up the ability to have more transparent conversations with your teams, is worth an experiment.

In this chapter, we've shared some concepts that leaders can start to deploy immediately that can increase organizational peripheral vision to expand the perceived playing field and become more familiar with new perspectives and ways of seeing the world. You can't see what you're blinded to, and you can't address what you can't see.

However, there's more to being a provocateur than just being able to identify trends. You have to know what to do with them when you find them. In Part II, we'll explore five strategies for what you can do when you discover a trend that impacts your organization. You'll see that there are multiple ways you can provoke – but how you do so depends highly on where you are in the "if-to-when" phase change . . . and whether you still have time and latitude to shape your future.

Part II

PRINCIPLES OF PROVOCATION

CHAPTER 5

Birth of a Provocation

"Don't provoke!"

This simple and clear admonishment was often heard around the Tuff household when Geoff and his five siblings were growing up. With a father who had a rich stable of go-to phrases passed down through generations of child-rearing Brits, the Tuff kids came to intuit what exactly was behind such short-and-sweet commands. This one was used primarily for the younger Tuffs when they were trying to get a rise out of their older brothers and sister.

Our guess is that similar scenes play out in many other households: a younger child takes action *just to see what will happen*. It could be a poke, or a verbal taunt, or the crafty hiding of a cherished item. Each one is intended just to see how far things can be pushed before a clobbering is administered.

That's how we learn about limits as kids – with our siblings, our parents, our friends, and even strangers. We try something and see what happens. And then we experience the results and learn what to do in the future.

For some reason, this inductive approach to learning wears off as we age. We grow up, learn lessons, and are taught generalizable rules. We make assumptions and rely on analogy to make use of experiences from the past, intuitively looking for ways to cut corners when making decisions. Gone is the natural instinct to act just to see what will happen – to *provoke*.

It's replaced by analysis, deduction, and a whole lot of thinking. That's a really bad character trait when you land in a world where lessons from the past are increasingly invalid.

RESPECT THE PAST, BUT HOLD IT LIGHTLY

In his 1905 book *Life of Reason*, the writer and philosopher George Santayana launched one of his most famous quotes: "Those who cannot remember the past are destined to repeat it." This makes sense to us as a general suggestion not to forget the lessons we have learned already: it is better to learn cumulatively than have to learn repeatedly. The problem is that most people seem to take it just a little too far, assuming that the past provides rock-solid guideposts about what the future holds, what is possible and what is not. Holding onto the past is one reason why we forget our inductive roots – and why we fail to provoke.

The bombing of Pearl Harbor and the terrorist attacks of 9/11 are two of the most ingrained stories of attacks by a foreign enemy on American soil in history. The tragic circumstances and outcomes of both resonated with people well beyond the United States and gave rise to some shared safety practices around the world. The attacks share a common thread: prevailing wisdom of the time, built on an understanding of the world, had been up to that point overshadowing the voices of those raising the alarm to the potential danger.

Many may be familiar with the failure to collate related intelligence warnings prior to the 9/11 attacks but are less aware that the attack on Pearl Harbor had its own warnings that were ignored. At the core of this breakdown was an idea – fueled by historical precedent, conventional wisdom, and basic racism – that the Japanese military simply did not have the wherewithal to attempt such an aggressive and ambitious operation.[1]

In the early 1940s, it was clear that the United States was on some sort of collision course with Japan. The Japanese had ambitions to modernize and challenge the West in industrial might, but a lack of natural resources on their island nation and overt American attempts to thwart their ambitions (by, for example, impeding the advance of the Japanese in China, freezing Japanese assets and tightening an embargo on the shipment of oil and other vital material) had slowed their progress. Early 1941 brought an American-educated admiral named Isoroku Yamamoto to the forefront of planning the surprise attack, a tactic the Japanese had used before in open hostilities with both China and Russia. This set up an imbalance: with a military leader more familiar with the West than many other Japanese leaders, and an American military leadership that was largely unversed in Eastern cultures, the ability to predict the future based on "knowledge" started to break down.

A full two decades earlier, an American military man named Billy Mitchell essentially predicted the attack in detail as part of a series of arguments he was making for the United States to establish an air force. Leading up to the attack on Pearl Harbor, American code experts successfully cracked encrypted messages between Tokyo and the Japanese emissaries in Washington, DC. These communications indicated that military action was likely forthcoming, and although some action was taken to move troops around and listen a little bit harder, the signals must have been largely discounted. On the morning of the attack, the 183 Japanese planes in the first wave of the attack were detected by radar, but officers rationalized away the spotting and assumed they were American planes returning to base.

With Pearl Harbor on low alert, aircraft were parked clustered together to prevent sabotage, and ammunition lockers were locked. Ninety minutes after the attack began, it was over, with devastating results: over 2,400 Americans, including civilians, were killed, more than an additional 100 injured, and 18 U.S. ships were sunk. The next day, America declared war on Japan.

The failure of the United States to anticipate and prepare for Pearl Harbor is a prime example of what happens when orthodoxy based on past experiences and embedded belief systems congeals to create an inability to act. As we saw in Part I, many boardrooms and C-suites are beset by the same issues. Our answer for what to do differently follows.

PROVOKE THE FUTURE

Our call to action for all leaders today is to DO SOMETHING! Provoke a better future – and, if you're a business, a better future means one in which you are advantaged. Whether that advantage is a competitive one held by your organization alone, or a socially oriented one in which the benefits accrue to many (higher and more equitable standards of living, less systemic racism, lower carbon emissions, and so on), the future we desire will likely not come to pass unless we have a hand in influencing it. It is up to us to provoke the future we want.

One common definition of "provoke" is "to cause reaction" – just like the Tuff kids used to do. But often a move to provoke is conceived as a singular action with at least a tinge of malicious intent. People are warned of wild animals that attack only when provoked, or of professional instigators – provocateurs – who stir up unrest in a crowd. We both think of and use the term in a much wider and more positive way.

To provoke is to take action with multiple different time-frames in mind. Small acts of provocation in the short term will create new knowledge and have a cumulative effect in the longer term. But all provocations take advantage of the fact that time is our scarcest resource. It is easy to convince ourselves that waiting until we have enough information to act is a safe move because we can, for example, either avoid wasting money on something that ultimately doesn't succeed or follow the lead of our competitors and end up with a comparable market position at a fraction of the cost. Unfortunately, as we've examined previously, because of several biases, humans have a bad habit of assuming the future is a linear extension of the past, and thereby also assuming that the same conditions will exist for the fast follower as existed for the first mover.

But by waiting and watching and collecting data, we are constantly wasting our time – using up one of the only currencies we know of that simply cannot be replaced, no matter how successful or well-funded we might be.

The trick – and the key to creating a better future – is to provoke with purpose. This chapter is intended to provide some ways of framing the provocation landscape in a way that goes beyond the simple notion of cause and effect.

As a first principle, our concept is intended to be causal. As such, it is different from many of the well-established decision-making methods in use around the world today that tend to be more reactive. Those models are based on the idea of gathering as much information as quickly as possible and incorporating that data into a continuous loop of decision-making and action.

The problem with those models is that the primacy of being able to act fast in the face of new information has natural limits. Although much has been made of the command centers of the likes of former New York City mayor Michael Bloomberg and Mark Zuckerberg – putting themselves in the heart of the action so that they can take in new information and act quickly – there are limits to the advantage they can create. We are trending toward a world of perfect and instant information. How and when we reach that point varies by industry and situation, but it appears inevitable that we will get there. It's a "when," not an "if." And when we do, the opportunity to create advantage via speed of response will present itself less and less frequently. That's why we need to learn how to provoke.

There are three key differences between the data-and-decide approaches and our idea of provocation. First, they rely on someone else as the primary actor or require new information as an instigation to act. That this has been the de facto approach to decision-making does not come as a surprise to us. Many business leaders have been brought up mired in the orthodoxy that "if it ain't broke, don't fix it." In other words, if you have no motivation to go and do things differently – whether that motivation comes in the form of new information, a competitive move, or an opportunity to take advantage of a new technology – then you might as well hold steady with the status quo.

The problem with this purely reactive approach to management is that it presumes that you can see the forces of change working around you. Historically, this has been largely true, with industry boundaries reasonably stable and sources (not to mention rate of flow) of information reasonably predictable. But with the rise of exponential change, those conditions disintegrate. If you leave it to someone else to be the first mover, or for new information to act as a lever to overcome organizational inertia, it is increasingly likely you'll be left behind.

Second, such data-driven approaches are all based on the notion that advantage can come from having better processing power and/or analytical techniques to make better use of new information. This compounds the first problem by focusing activity and management attention on analysis. Perversely, in the face of potential disruption, many turn inward and seek more data and more confidence in what the algorithms are telling them, instead of outward to understand the new forces of change at play. If we rely on better insight through better analytical techniques, inevitably the focus turns to higher and higher burdens of proof instead of a push to look at the world differently.

Third, they presume that lessons from the past can guide action in the future. By definition, all data is retrospective. It's a good way to take risk out of decisions that approximate those that we have faced in the past, but it's useless in facing the brand new or the wholly uncertain. The only way to add contours and "knowability" to an uncertain situation is to provoke a reaction in your market – in the broadest sense of that word: the field of play that you're on – by taking action.

This bias for action is at the very heart of thinking like a provocateur. At every step of the provocation, you will likely need to check the natural instinct to collect more data and do more analysis and instead to just go DO SOMETHING!

The interesting thing about a bias for action is that it appears to be innate. Faced with something that appears suddenly dangerous, our amygdalas are wired to start firing to kick off the fight-or-flight response, releasing adrenaline, which enables or accelerates action. Many of us have probably seen an overly dramatic movie clip, or read a scene from a novel, or even a funny cartoon in which one character screams to another to "do something!" in the face of imminent danger: a stove fire, an approaching bear, a weird sound in the night. The reality of a proximate physical threat is enough to spur action and dispatch with the analysis. The chosen action may not be the right call in the moment but, if it isn't, the protagonist will learn (inductively) and try something different.

Why is it, then, that in business settings that are no less existential in nature, hardly anyone ever screams, "Do something!" Instead, the caricature in a parallel movie, novel, or cartoon would show someone thoughtfully leaning back in his chair and asking a subordinate – in a very measured way – to "run the numbers again" or "go study X." Is this scenario different from the first one because the existential threat is to the business rather than to the person? Or is it because the threat feels less proximate? Either way, we all need to start building muscles that will help us overcome these barriers to just take action in the business setting.

KNOWING HERE FROM THERE

Acting with purpose is impossible unless you know where you are and – roughly – where you would like to be. That doesn't necessarily mean always having a comprehensive view of your optimal future. But it does mean knowing what constitutes the most critical aspects of your desired state and what uncertainties will impact the likelihood of it coming to pass. For example, consider these desired states:

- If market demand for desalination in India takes off due to rising sea levels to [this level] by [this date], I am well-positioned to make a killing if I invest in brine technologies today.

- If population growth in Africa represents roughly half the global population increase set to occur over the next ~30 years, venture bets placed by large tech companies (and others) will likely result in substantial returns.[2]

- If the cost of travel to outer space continues to fall over the coming decades, certain industries (e.g., mining of heavy metals and minerals) can place bets to take advantage of this new frontier.[3]

The key is to be able to frame your desired state in sufficient detail so that you can name the uncertainties. As discussed in Part I, what distinguishes successful provocateurs from timid analysts is the confidence to act and the ability to recognize the phase change as a trend solidifies to become inevitable – that is, when you stop asking "if" something is going to happen and start asking "when" – and what the trend means for you. That is one of the most important factors to consider as you choose how to provoke.

THE PROVOKE QUINTET

We have organized Part II around five general models of provocation. We are going to introduce them here and then dive into much more detail with real-life examples in subsequent chapters.

1. Envision: The foundational provocation that allows you to see the future(s) that could emerge over time.

2. Position: Situate your organization to take advantage of the emerging future(s).

3. Drive: Directly create an impact that is advantageous to you.

4. Adapt: Shift your business model to best fit the inevitable outcomes, moving as quickly as possible to create advantage.

5. Activate: Trigger a network or knock-on effect – often through an ecosystem – that stands the highest chance of leading to your desired outcome.

Envision: The Foundational Provocation

There is only one provocation that should be treated as a constant, episodic action, an active and ongoing move, and that's envision. Where are you on the rollercoaster tracks? How big and steep is the upcoming hill, and when will the trend tip over into kinetic action? The idea is to keep this as organic as possible; you want to keep changing the focus of the learning based on what you discover along the way. This foundational activity of charting a course should be dynamically adjusted as new information becomes available. As soon as you find yourself doing the same analysis by rote, over and over again, you'll know you are dangerously close to solidifying playbooks that will need to be detonated.

Part of what it takes to envision is simply to have a bead on your desired outcome, along with the uncertainties involved in its unfolding. More importantly, the most powerful envision moves involve the development of multiple scenarios or stories of how the future *could* unfold, along with leading indicators that help give notice when the relative likelihood of any given scenario goes up or down. We will explore this concept – and the right versus wrong ways of scenario planning – in the next chapter.

Position: Preparing for the Future You'll Create

When facing a trend in the "if" phase – that is, when it is still genuinely uncertain whether the phase change will ever become inevitable – the key is to position yourself to explore as the trend starts to reveal its true colors. Although there are multiple ways a trend can move into the "when" phase, there are really only two categories that matter. Either (a) it happens naturally, meaning that the leading indicators of one future scenario align in a way to push it through to the "when" phase without direct intervention; or (b) it happens synthetically due to actions that you or others take.

For an example of natural resolution, consider the world's environment. It now appears inevitable that the period of uncertainty related to whether humans would take climate change seriously has naturally resolved into only a question of time before decarbonization becomes pervasive. An increase in data and insight, the rise of a variety of extreme weather events, and a growing chorus of voices demanding action have all conspired to drive the phase change, though it's difficult to point to one actor or one event that catalyzed the outcome. We will delve into this topic in much more detail in the next chapter, but it is worth using this space to point out that ignorance is not the same as uncertainty. For some period of time, the world was simply unaware that the burning of fossil fuels caused the release of greenhouse gases and contributed to global warming. Call it blindness or obliviousness, but for most trends you can find a pre-uncertainty origination stage where no one had even laid a hypothesis on the table that something might be a possible reality.

Synthetic resolution *does* have a primary cause. Sometimes a single visionary drives the resolution, but increasingly it takes an ecosystem of individuals or companies working together to provoke the world in which they are advantaged. Some of the most famed tech giants fall into this category: Bill Gates, Steve Jobs, Elon Musk, and Mark Zuckerberg can all be credited to have been at the heart of the phase change that created some of the best-known technology trends. These are the obvious provocateurs. As we delve into the provoke quintet in more detail in late chapters, we will explore some lesser-known examples from outside the world of tech.

In the "if" phase one must act to discover three pieces of critical information. The first piece is early awareness that leading indicators are resolving in one direction or another: this helps the provocateur understand where you sit on the rollercoaster, and, importantly, if you are entering the "if-to-when" phase change. The second piece is clarity around the degree to which you have the ability to influence the eventuality of your desired outcome (e.g., what degree of influence do you have in the system? What constraints – regulatory, technical, and so forth – exist? How direct is the causality / how sensitive is the trigger you might act on?). The third is the complexity of the pathway that leads to your desired outcome: How many actors need to be involved? Over what period of time will the pathway unfold? What interdependencies exist? Collectively, the provocative moves in this bucket constitute *active* sensing rather than a passive "wait and see" mode which is the unfortunate common default when faced with uncertainty.

Once you've reached a perspective on the important information to gather, the provocateur must take three important steps. First, place bets – by diversifying your portfolio of investments – based on your current relative belief in each of the future scenarios coming true. Some of those bets will be "no regret" bets that create advantage in all of the scenarios; some of them will necessarily constitute a spreading of the chips to account for a variety of possible outcomes.

The second step is to design and prepare for the execution of a test in a way that it gives you isolated data on a hypothesis. Test design is critically important; the purpose is not to see if you can "make money" or succeed broadly. You are trying to get early indications of whether you can impact the behavior of the market in a way that creates a better future for you. The biggest mistake most companies make in this step is framing a test so broadly that when results come in there's too much noise to be confident in the next move.

Finally, act to see if you can trigger a reaction from the market you are focused on, whether that is an external or an internal one. This could involve watching the reaction to a prototype via pilot test, or seeing if you can trigger a reaction from extreme users by announcing an intended offer. But the act of testing always needs to be observational and aimed at watching for an actual behavior as opposed to asking the market, "What would you do if X happens?"

Drive and Adapt

The Drive and Adapt provocations can, in theory, rest largely on any organization's belief that it, and it alone, is in control of its destiny – a situation that is typically marked by low complexity. Said differently, the degree to which the company will succeed or fail in the potential future is largely determined by its own actions. These are the provocations that allow you to act in a way that creates advantage in a world that you know is going to come true . . . even if you don't know exactly when.

Where drive and adapt differ is the degree to which you have the ability to impact the trend. In situations where you can influence the speed or shape of when the phase change will happen, then you would use the drive provocation strategy to take action to shape the trend to your advantage (think of a company working with regulators on a new product or service). In adapt, while you are still able to shape your own destiny, you believe you can't have influence on the trend itself in a way that is perfectly consistent with your existing business model; you just need to reshape your organization to take advantage of the trend (a good example is companies positioning themselves to take advantage of market growth in the so-called "BRIC" markets several years back).

Activate

You might conclude from the above paragraph that drive is a more powerful form of provocation than adapt and, therefore, it should be "preferred." It might indeed be true that if you can shape your environment to your advantage, you should do so. Unfortunately, we think it's an increasingly rare situation where a single actor can meaningfully shape the direction of a trend. The world is more and more interconnected and actions to shape the future require multiple actors to have impact. That's where the Activate provocation comes in. If you're acting early enough in the phase change, but can't impact the trend alone, you'll need to work to activate an ecosystem of others to have impact. This could be either formal and overt moves to engage an ecosystem, or more informal ones where you are more subtly signaling intent to others.

SUMMING UP

These provocation strategies are not mutually exclusive. In fact, against any individual trend, an organization could use multiple provocations as the trend moves through the "if-to-when" phase change. The key is to match the provocation to the trend.

The purpose of a provoke mindset is to enable a series of *minimally viable moves* that continuously shape the trend as it unfolds. It's unlikely that the path to provoking a better future is a smooth arc. Rather, it's likely to require multiple small recalibrations along the way. The best strategy is a continuous learning process of aiming-acting-learning against the trend, understanding the nature of the impact you are able to have on a given trend and leveraging minimally viable moves to make forward progress. As an important note, "minimally viable" is a relative term. Some industries by their nature require larger bets. Consider the difference in scale of deciding whether to build a petrochemical refinery overseas versus testing a new marketing message in a limited, local market. The important thing for any leader is to make the minimally viable move as small as it can be in order to sufficiently test the hypothesis at hand.

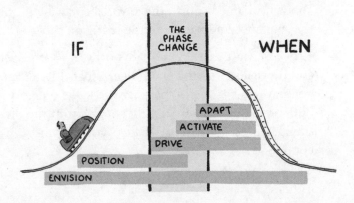

The most critical thing to get right in crafting a path forward is to have an initial hypothesis about how any move will play out in the market. Comparing actual with anticipated results will allow you to move all the more quickly to the next minimally viable move and will also help you understand when "enough is enough" within any given step.

It is important to update your initial hypothesis based on learning from your actions. This will involve considering the following four components:

1. What is the degree of certainty you have about the likely reaction in the market? Are you more or less confident about what is likely to happen, or is this mainly an opportunity to build knowledge?

2. What is the likely speed of the feedback loop in any given test? Some situations are inherently slower to send signals back (due to velocity of market activity, transaction cycle time, etc.), and a portfolio of tests that are only long-term in nature may unnecessarily slow forward progress.

3. What is the likely signal-to-noise ratio in the data you get back from the market? There will be some noise in almost any response so having an initial perspective about how much noise there will be can help guide the sequence and nature of the tests you run.

4. What is the value creation hypothesis (both upside and downside) behind the move? That doesn't mean you have to know exactly what the value equation is, but you should be sufficiently confident in the directional source of value or risk so you can move with confidence.

As we will explore in subsequent chapters, individuals and companies who have effectively designed provocation strategies don't actually know the exact route that will unfold as they pursue their desired future. In fact, more often than not, surprises along the way require them to redirect, but they all have a constant North Star that guides their day-to-day decisions and action. And they all keep moving forward, shunning over-analysis and deduction in favor of induction: learning along the way as they get out and DO SOMETHING!

CHAPTER 6

Envision: Seeing
the Future

One of us is an avid sailor. By *avid*, we don't mean "America's-Cup-winning" or "singlehanded across the Atlantic – in winter." Rather, he likes to spend as much time as he can out on the water in the warmer months, toddling around in a daysailer with a cooler of beverages until life's regular responsibilities call him back to shore.

Sailors loom large in the public imagination – some mythologized, some cursed – but to us they hold a fascination because they are natural scenario planners. Whether you've been sailing for 5 years or 50, when you're anticipating getting out on the water you start to pay attention to things: what the weather forecast is calling for; low and high tide times along with average tide levels; average wind speed and gust ranges; sunset, sunrise, and moon phase. The list goes on. In time, some of this knowledge – or the act of updating it – becomes innate. The need to check the tide charts lessens as we just check the water levels on the way to and from the morning coffee run. Or we watch the patterns of the neighbor's flags for signs of what kind of sailing day it's likely to be based on a decade of watching the same flags, out the same window, at the same time of day.

As we head out on the water, this base load of information provides a context for how we might expect the sail to go – but nothing more than a context. Every sail is different due to the small, unforeseen shifts in the weather, wind, and waves.

And when underway, experienced sailors almost pathologically scan. They look for darker water to indicate slightly heavier wind and shimmering water low on waves to indicate a lull. They look at and for other boats around them – sometimes to avoid running into them, often just to assess how they are sailing on a relative basis. They look for shifts in the cloud formations and especially the turning of cumulus clouds into cumulonimbus clouds, which suggests that some uncertainty around a fair-weather day has resolved into a trend toward a thunderstorm.

Watch the average experienced sailor in the face of this new and evolving data and you will see them work through an ever-evolving series of tweaks and adjustments of sail trim and direction. And if you happen to be on board during a high-stakes race, the lines involved and physicality and verbalization of what needs to happen grow exponentially. The act of sailing is – almost by definition – an act of taking what you thought you knew about the way the day was going to turn out and throwing it out the window piece by piece as you receive more information and adjust course as necessary. But, most of the time, although the journey is not at all what had been specifically planned, the destination – a safe berth at a targeted port – is exactly as desired since all new information gathered enables the skipper to get evermore precise about the movements he needs to make to achieve his goal.

But not all the time.

Indeed, sailing is not always sunshine and steady breezes. Sometimes things go really, really badly. Tales of sailing disasters abound and puzzlingly many of them have involved experienced sailors. As we started to pick through these stories, we started to notice a common theme. Although certainly not true of every sailing tragedy, many shared the trait that the sailors involved tended toward over reliance on past experience. They discounted the data in front of them and often questioned their own senses, and instead adhered to a narrative about how the sail was going to turn out that they simply wanted to believe. They forgot to adjust assumptions to incorporate new information and to make ever-more-precise decisions about what to do next.

They forgot to be scenario planners.

One particularly poignant story unfolded on Mobile Bay, in the Gulf of Mexico, in 2015. At the time that events occurred, the Dauphin Island race had been run for over half a century. Sailed on a one-way route down and through the mouth of Mobile Bay, the annual tradition had involved perhaps tens of thousands of sailors over time. Lessons of all sorts had been learned and passed down through the generations. This time, it was *partly on account of* those lessons that things went seriously awry. Due to the simultaneous strike of three unpredicted and unpredictable storm cells at once, close to a dozen boats were destroyed; 40 sailors had to be rescued from the water; and six people, ranging in age from their teenage years to over 70, lost their lives.[1]

At the heart of the disaster was an overreliance on past patterns of weather behavior and overconfidence in individual ability to react in the moment. Although the race participants had been warned of unsettled weather as they headed into the race, only 8 of the 125 boats dropped out. But what those who remained experienced simply had no precedent. There were none of the giveaway swirls on the weather radar to suggest gathering strong winds. There was none of the usual time to spot and then react to a surprise change in weather by getting quickly to shore. Instead of the normal trend for severe storms to quickly blow themselves out, these seemed only to intensify as they cut through the racecourse. In an instant, everything the sailors "knew" changed.

Much has been written over time about the impact of black-swan events and how, with the benefit of hindsight, even the most unpredictable events can seem like they could have been accounted for. Arguably, the Mobile Bay disaster fits the profile of such an event. Although most ex post facto black-swan explanation involves piecing together leading indicators viewed retrospectively, the best provocateurs can do the same prospectively. Always paying keen attention to the signals we know matter most, and using those to expand the aperture to account for even the most outlandish outcomes allows the best provocateurs – the best scenario planners – to make evermore precise predictions about what is to come and to adjust course accordingly. Sometimes that adjustment requires a wholesale abandonment of previous plans.

The great mistake that sailors made on Mobile Bay that day was to assume they were facing the same weather trends that they had grown accustomed to, rather than a newly uncertain reality. They forgot to be scenario planners.

THE FUNDAMENTALS OF ENVISION

The envision provocation sets our context for moving forward. Many aspects of what it means to envision effectively have direct parallels with our sailing analogy:

- It represents the foundational activity of charting a course.

- It must be dynamically adjusted as new information becomes available.

- Especially early in the experience journey, it may require a discrete or one-off effort to build the baseload information, but over time it will become continuous and (more) innate.

- It is critical that you learn in the moment and adjust assumptions taken from lessons from the past; don't assume you are simply executing a routine that will always be governed by the same externalities in the same way.

Any successful envisioning exercise will allow you to accomplish three things. First, it will help you understand your frame of reference through a desired outcome. Second, it will help you develop scenarios and place initial bets. Third, it will enable you to identify signposts and leading indicators of how the future is unfolding to track over time, setting yourself up to course correct as necessary.

One cautionary note: you *absolutely should not* turn scenario planning into a rote process that is repeated just because "it's that time of year." Most well-intended decision-making protocols that worked at one point in time become defunct once they get turned into a process-driven playbook. If you've read our other work, you know that we are no fans of playbooks. This is a surefire way to miss the nuance in the signals around you as you focus on executing the steps in the process.

We were asked recently whether this abhorrence of process means that we do not believe in the value of – for example – making lists. Perhaps one of the best-known treatises on the value of lists comes from the world of medicine: Atul Gawande's *The Checklist Manifesto*. We love this book and absolutely support the value that lists can provide in reducing what Gawande calls "errors of ineptitude." But this only works if the issue at hand is *known or knowable*. Procedures (medical or otherwise) with precedent where we can reasonably rely on data from the past can absolutely have error rates reduced – though probably not eliminated – through using checklists. Our argument is simply that, increasingly, the world around us and the decisions we make in it are not knowable; you can't

know what's on the other side of the rollercoaster's peak. In the face of the unknown and unknowable, you need scenarios – not checklists – to serve as the foundation for action. This is at the heart of what it takes to envision.

In no way should envisioning be confused with a bias to "wait and see." We are still dealing with that most precious currency of time, and we should be feeling constantly antsy to DO SOMETHING!

ENVISIONING THE FUTURE OF ENERGY

The best way to demonstrate the power of scenario thinking is to move through an example that illuminates how it is different than a typical "upside and downside" exercise. We can think of no better issue to tackle through the lens of envisioning than the future of energy, which has multiple powerful forces that influence how the world could evolve.

It is not news that the question of how we address climate change has been one of the most intractable issues of the modern era. Squabbling about "what the science says," interwoven into politics and partisanship, seems thankfully to be largely centered in the United States. Most of the world now takes as a fact that our climate is changing; that humans are at least one central cause; that with climate change comes an increasing global average temperature, greater temperature swings, and more extreme weather events; and that we can impact the trend lines by taking action. Interestingly, it took the 2020 COVID-19 pandemic and the subsequent collapse in demand for travel and fossil fuels to convince some of these reasonably straightforward matters of common sense.

Sadly, the world got stuck for far too long on this surface layer of arguing about observable phenomena. Recently, Geoff and a number of our colleagues spent time thinking about whether there might be a way to use scenarios to break through this surface layer. We are using that thinking in a summarized and stylized way throughout this chapter to demonstrate the power of scenarios.[2]

Let's start with an important premise – we believe that many of the reports and predictions about climate change are insufficient to enable action for a lot of organizations. As of early 2020, prepandemic, the colloquial term for the collective set of anticipated changes was known as the "energy transition." People saw this as a period of decarbonization as we shifted from carbon-based energy sources to cleaner and more renewable sources. But beyond that acknowledgment lay a vast field of uncertainty on multiple dimensions.

To be clear, plenty of data, analysis, projections, and thousands upon thousands of reports intended to clarify a path forward have been created. Indeed, the sheer volume of information is, in and of itself, almost paralyzing. But little of this collective knowledge leaves us feeling well equipped to think through how to create a better future through the energy transition. It is also clear that these choices are relevant for literally everyone: for people (that is, humans living with climate change and its implications, citizens putting pressure on governments, consumers, businesspeople), for businesses (both those in the energy production and transmission industries and those that consume energy as a critical component of their operations), and for governments (regulators, policy makers, diplomats, and so on).

Many climate change studies fall prey to some combination of three significant deficiencies that anyone with a genuine intent to envision a better future needs to work beyond.

First, they represent sensitivity analyses, not scenarios. For decades, there have been standard measures of climate change. Simple metrics like temperature, rainfall, and wind speed help explain the nature of our climate at any moment. Thus, time-series data can signal change rates over time. The Paris Climate Accords of 2016 were based on a multinational alignment to "keep the increase in global average temperature to well below 2 °C (3.6 °F) above preindustrial levels; and to pursue efforts to limit the increase to 1.5 °C (2.7 °F), recognizing that this would substantially reduce the risks and impacts of climate change."[3] Some folks' arguments against science notwithstanding, these are indeed simple metrics to track and communicate. The problem is that they are so simple that they are distracting.

What the world came to know as scenarios for climate change were not real scenarios that work to explain outcomes across sometimes dozens of uncertainties simultaneously. Instead, they focused on ranges of possible outcomes *along single vectors of projection* (frequently global average temperature), simplifying away the interconnectedness of other variables. This approach creates two sets of blinders for managers: (1) it does not account for the nuance of causality in their forward-looking plans, and (2) it warps the perception of what management systems are most important to run the company. As an example of the causality point, imagine if average temperature drops by 100 basis points because catastrophic weather events trigger a financial collapse due to insurance exposure. The opportunities and risks for any company in that future state are likely to be dramatically different from one in which average temperature drops by 100 basis points because a breakthrough in green hydrogen technology makes it viable as a fuel substitute across a range of transport applications.

Let's use a fictitious company to illustrate the point about management systems. The company DecarbPLUS builds a product that is particularly attractive for markets with higher-than-average CO_2 emissions per capita. Typically, in trying to decide when to enter a certain market, they would logically build a model to forecast CO_2 emissions – and the output of the model would invariably be a dominant trend line representing the base case with a range on either side of it showing upside and downside to this expected case (usually in a relatively narrow band). That image would then be almost destined to become the obsessive focus of management and their analysts trying to decide whether to enter the market; after all, as the adage goes, "What gets measured gets managed." And slowly they will start to refer to points within the range of possible outcomes as "scenarios."

But as with any phenomenon governed by uncertainty, many other factors – many other vectors – play a role and must be considered. And many of those factors might in fact be interrelated such that changes in one vector unpredictably influence another. The legacy of deductive thinking has left us

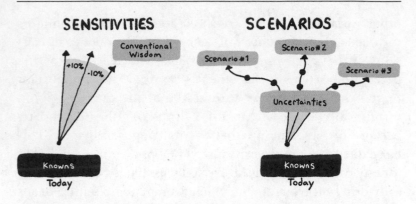

with an obsession with precision and a desire to learn from the past to build models that predict the future. In many arenas – including the one surrounding the topic of climate change – that is literally computationally impossible given the number of variables involved. Perversely, instead of acknowledging this and looking for a better way to frame the future, many organizations turn a blind eye to this complexity and instead pick their favorite metric or two to harp on. The end result is a narrow extension of the past that leaves the organization blind to discontinuities.

There is in fact a better way.

A real scenario analysis considers multiple different uncertainties simultaneously, consolidating differing resolution of the uncertainties into a plausible *story* of what the future could look like. Often that story takes the form of a qualitative narrative, but the most effective scenario discussions combine stories with quantitative modeling to describe connections and collinearities between uncertainties *from a future-back perspective*. Of course, any scenario always needs to be considered relative to alternative, equally plausible scenarios in which the resolution of the uncertainties is different. Building scenarios is at the heart of the envision provocation.

Second, most studies stop short of the most fundamental drivers of outcomes. As anyone who pays any attention to climate debates is well aware, the two central questions that weigh on everyone's minds are (1) whether renewable technology will advance fast enough and affordably enough to present a viable alternative to fossil fuels, and (2) whether governments will artificially impact the rate of decarbonization for some period of time using regulations and incentives – tax incentives for renewable adoption, carbon pricing, trade regulation, and so on. These are indeed two important considerations, but they don't get to the *actual* root-cause drivers of outcomes in the energy system.

Government intervention and technological innovation fit better in the category of outcome, rather than causal factor, even if the outcome is not an end-market outcome. There is no amount of innovation and no amount of governmental influence that is impossible with the right demand conditions in place. Just think back to 2020 and how fast we got to multiple effective vaccines for COVID-19. With focused resources and prioritization, coupled with government support, the timeline was reduced to months from years. In other words, if society is aligned on the need for decarbonization – lobbying for it, willing to pay for it, aiming their R&D resources at it in the business domain – then it will happen. Yes, there will be some regions of the world where the balance of supply and demand is skewed by government intervention, but not enough to prevent global progress, especially if we live in a world with some degree of international collaboration.

These root-cause drivers – societal reaction and government collaboration – are therefore a better way to frame competing outcomes: a way for players in the market to see new options and opportunities to create advantage through the energy transition instead of getting hung up on factors that feel largely out of their control.

There are likely a lot of reasons why the world has gotten hung up on policy and technology as barriers (or enablers) to the energy transition. They are tangible and trackable. They are somewhat predictable – or at least they feel that way. There are precedents for action that we can use to assign probabilities for the future. There are people and organizations who one can communicate with to gain confidence that we know the development curve either is on. The problem is all these reasons presume that we can rely on historical data and past action as a guide for the future. As we know, that's a dangerous presumption when dealing with multiple vectors of uncertainty simultaneously.

The third and perhaps most important shortfall of most studies is that they haven't driven substantive action. The biggest problem with most of the world's perspectives on the future of energy is that they are useful for only a very small set of organizations. Energy policy makers have felt well tended because they have been given a treasure trove of data to sift through and interpret in ways that best fit their purposes. But for the average leader, the only conclusion that could be drawn has been, "Well, I guess we'll just have to wait and see."

To make something more actionable for current leaders, we need to insert them, personally, into the timeline. Most of what we see uses projections to 2050 or beyond based on targets and commitment dates in multinational agreements, driven by the need to promote agreement. Everyone can agree on something that is well into the future, right? The problem is, it doesn't create a platform to DO SOMETHING right now. The right timeframe for consideration should be far enough so that the uncertainties could genuinely resolve in different ways but close enough in for managers to feel urgency to start to take action today. For the future of energy, we believe that's 15 years.

We highlight three steps through our energy example:

1. Create a focal question that allows for consideration of a diversity of desired outcomes.

2. Develop scenarios and place initial bets.

3. Identify leading indicators to track over time, correcting course as necessary.

Create a Focal Question That Allows for Consideration of a Diversity of Desired Outcomes

In corporate competitive strategy, a desired outcome is usually framed as a future in which the company is advantaged. When it comes to something as wide reaching as the future of energy, however, the desired outcome will vary wildly depending on the constituent in question. The policy maker might desire an outcome that demonstrates that the Paris Accords are not as unattainable as some would argue. The utility player might desire a state in which the new energy system requires as little retrofitting of their existing infrastructure as possible. The anticarbon environmentalist might desire an outcome in which all oil and gas supermajors either go out of business or shut down all their extraction activities in favor of a different business model. And said oil and gas supermajor might desire a future in which the tail to fossil fuel use is as long as possible.

The trick is to effectively translate your desired state into as concrete a focal question for consideration in your scenario development as possible, one that specifically addresses the decision you need to make. It should allow for flexibility to explore the rosiest of plausible scenarios you desire but also encompass alternative futures that do not work in your favor.

For this example, we suggest a broad focal question like, "How will the energy system evolve by 2035, and how might this affect the extended energy ecosystem?"

Develop Scenarios and Place Initial Bets

The actual scenario development – especially the first run through it – is the most time-intensive part of envisioning. As with the sailor who eventually can glance at tide charts only episodically in favor of using her own observations of the sea level, we are confident that the rigor required to update and evolve scenarios will decline over time, but only if the initial foundation put in place is robust.

The objective of this activity will feel foreign for many who are used to analysis as a means to gain courage to act. Most organizations prize the ability to see into the future with certainty through ever-more sophisticated access to data and analytical techniques. For the increasingly complex environment in which most companies operate today, that's simply not possible. Instead, the purpose of scenarios is to "imagine with confidence" rather than bulletproof certainty. Good scenarios have built into them a sense of humility that the only thing we will end up knowing about them for certain is that none of them will be what actually ends up happening. However, designed correctly, they will be sufficiently believable and detailed that they motivate action to set off on the journey, much like a day out on the water.

At the heart of good scenarios lies a comprehensive understanding of all the driving forces that might impact the desired outcome and focal question. Those forces must be sorted and narrowed to focus only on the forces that will have meaningful impact on the focal question, honestly and confidently declare which of them are already in the "when" phase and should not be treated as uncertain (except regarding timing), and result in a subset of the highest-impact forces that are genuinely uncertain (i.e., in the "if" stage).

There are many plausible forces to consider. Geoff and his colleagues got up to 92 potential driving forces based on research and perspectives from leading thinkers. A closer look at that long list, though, suggests that some are interesting but not really impactful to the focal question. They could serve as red herrings in the envision exercise. Of the remaining items, while some are genuinely in the "if" phase of uncertainty, others have already crossed the phase to change to "when" (or, in this example, "at what rate"). These include, for example, the following:

- Global energy demand will continue to increase but the growth rate will continue to decline.

- Technological innovation will continue.

- Decarbonization will be a global imperative.

- Global economic and population growth will increase.

- Emissions will slow, but not to target levels by 2035.

Although there still may be some debate in pockets around the world on whether these are givens, Geoff and his colleagues decided that further debate would be a distraction. They instead chose to focus on what they thought mattered: the 19 remaining uncertainties, the "ifs," that fell into five buckets related to social, technological, environmental, economic, and political trends. Some examples of these include the following:

- How will the advent of new technologies and processes impact end use demand for energy?

- Will the voice of individuals, banded together, meaningfully impact abatement curves?

- What is the likely nature of future international collaboration on a variety of fronts (economic, climate related, social, etc.)?

- What will happen to hydrocarbon financing and/or access to capital for companies resting on a carbon-based business model?

Across those 19, the nature of their uncertainty varies, especially as they relate to the 2035 timeframe they were considering. Some show signs of being in phase change between "if" and "when," but the critical remaining uncertainty is whether that phase change will happen by 2035. Examples include the existence of qualified talent to build and operate a decarbonized infrastructure, rate of improvement in energy storage, and sustained action to address climate change. Others they anticipated would remain solidly in the "if" phase for the foreseeable future – society and the customer's voice, for example, and access to essential raw materials.

Once Geoff and his colleagues had their uncertainties chosen, they created the scenario frame. This is one of the most critical choices in scenario planning, combining two uncertainties to frame the scenarios. The original scenario planning professionals – a group that emerged from Shell in the 1970s and eventually became the consulting service Global Business Network – found long ago that no matter what innovation one might try to apply to the approach, the good old 2×2 actually works best here. This will result in four discrete and, ideally, mutually exclusive and collectively exhaustive (MECE) versions of the future.

For those of you who might desire to complicate things further by suggesting there really is a third important axis, trust us; adding another dimension to the 2×2 will create mind-boggling complexity, making it nearly impossible to build, explain, and take action against. The challenge is to select or create two axes that connect with the most fundamental drivers of outcomes, create the most explanatory power across all the uncertainties, and are likely to maintain their explanatory value over time and in a variety of settings, even though the relative likelihood of any of the scenarios they frame may shift.

For the future of energy, the two that best met these criteria are related to society's voice in response to climate change and the degree of international economic collaboration, as depicted in the 2×2 scenario image.

On the *y*-axis, which frames the endpoints of "proactive" versus "reactive" response to climate change, *society* refers not only to consumers as is typically conceived (i.e., "will consumers demand green value chains and be willing to pay a price premium accordingly?"), but also businesspeople and government workers who are in a position to exert influence in other ways. And the *x*-axis, which frames the nature and depth of international economic collaboration, is meant to go well beyond policy influence and describe different outcomes in terms of degree of capital flow, whether new technology standards are set and shared, collaboration in terms of shared IP and access to raw materials, and so on.

SCENARIOS FOR THE FUTURE OF ENERGY

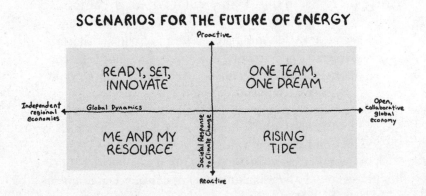

What results from using these axes are four discrete, equally plausible versions for how the future of energy may evolve through 2035.

Good scenarios – beyond hanging together as a collection – must pass muster across three tests. First, one needs to be able to write a compelling narrative – a story – that brings to life the scenario and how it has come to be in a way that is generally believable (if not desired) by varied audiences. Second, you must be able to explain how all critical uncertainties resolve in the scenario. Third, ideally, every scenario must have a quantitative model behind it that is generally "plug compatible" with most planning and tracking systems, using common metrics and referencing widely acknowledged baselines. For the future-of-energy exercise, quantitative models had to include metrics like "total primary energy demand" and "share of renewables in electricity consumption," which can be compared to baselines established by organizations like the International Energy Agency.

For an example of what we mean by a narrative, let's take the "One Team, One Dream" scenario that Geoff and his colleagues developed, in which society's voice is proactive in demanding wide-scale and accelerated decarbonization and we are living in a world characterized by global collaboration on a variety of fronts. In this (highly summarized) scenario:

> Imagine a world united after a series of climate shocks, collaborating and growing in a way we have not yet seen. Consumer behavior dramatically favors the long-term health and environmental, economic, and social benefit of the collective, triggering a globally collaborative atmosphere that successfully commercializes low-carbon technology and commits to drastic decarbonization. Fierce competition exists between energy companies to scale accessible, low-carbon technologies to meet consumer demand. Tech players invest in efficiencies up the value chain to reduce the impact of widely used products.

Governments open borders to allow for a web of connected services and introduce a global carbon-pricing mechanism.

Identify Leading Indicators to Track Over Time, Enabling Course Correction as Necessary

The final stage of a good envision provocation establishes what we should be paying attention to as we manage through the face of uncertainty. These are leading indicators (primarily quantitative) and signposts (primarily qualitative) that we need to build sensing systems to monitor in an increasingly intuitive way over time. Think of the "pathological scan" of the sailor, constantly taking in new information – but only from the most relevant sources – to change course as necessary.

As a collection, these indicators and signposts provide the backbone of a sensing system that will be one of the best sources of information about when uncertainties are resolving into trends. For example, indicators for the "One Team, One Dream" scenario would include the following:

- Global GDP growth running at roughly 2–3% (vs., for example, 1.5–2.5% for Ready, Set, Innovate)

- Major climate shocks in developed nations

- Share of renewables in electricity generation hitting 50–55% by 2025 (vs., for example, 35–40% for Rising Tide)

- Adoption of electric vehicles accelerating around the world (rather than in pockets) and at greater than prior rates

- Gross fixed capital formation increasing globally through 2035

These are just a few of the signals that Geoff and his Envisioneers decided they had to pay attention to right now so they could continue to sharpen how they envision the future of energy and its impact on climate change. The good news is that the team will continue to gain access to ever-more-sophisticated systems to monitor these signposts and indicators, increasingly in real time. As the future unfolds, the hope and belief is that all organizations will be able to react with increasing intuition as information flows become as natural as a sailor's sense of how the weather is unfolding.

What they do with that information will depend, of course, on their desired outcome.

CHAPTER 7

Position: Preparing for the Change

O nce upon a time, Geoff quit his job, sold everything he owned, asked a girl he had just started dating to do the same, and set off hitchhiking, not to return for a year. True story , , , ish.

That's actually the abbreviated, somewhat apocryphal version of the story of an experiment that really did happen. The slightly longer, slightly truer version is more complicated.

Geoff had been working in his consulting job for just over a year after college when he started to get antsy and worried that he had thrown away a life of writing and bohemian wandering to Grateful Dead shows in favor of a corporate world that he still didn't feel comfortable in. Reflecting back on a visit the previous summer from a college friend – nicknamed the Elf – who had just finished backpacking around the world, Geoff couldn't get out of his mind the idea that maybe he should do something similar and give writing another try.

In the early 1990s, the world travel scene was markedly different from today's. There were no cell phones and thus no way to communicate with loved ones back home outside of expensive, hurried payphone calls or vellum-thin airmail letters written in a micro-font. There was no widespread use of personal computers, let alone travel sites to learn about possible destinations and current political conditions – just word-of-mouth stories swapped in hostels with other travelers or out-of-date *Lonely Planet* books. And there definitely were no money-back satisfaction guarantees forced by the risk of exposure on social media. The Elf's core pieces of advice to Geoff made sense: "Always have a Plan B, and don't plan too much."

As luck would have it, Geoff had recently started dating a woman who was due to graduate from college the following spring and who had not yet nailed down postgraduation plans. They started talking and eventually hatched a scheme. In essence, they were going to design an experiment that served two purposes simultaneously. First, they wanted to understand whether their relationship had what it took to stand the test of time. Second, they wanted to understand whether Geoff had it in him to focus on writing in a way that suggested he could make a living from it. At a minimum, they wanted to put in place mechanisms to test whether they were in the early stage of a phase change from "if" to "when" on both fronts. Ideally, they wanted to see if they could catalyze that phase change.

With the Elf's advice guiding them, they crafted a trip on which they would spend a year backpacking around the world, always with a plan B in mind if anything – large or small – didn't turn out as expected. They picked certain destinations that both liked the look of but also kept individual lists that contained places that didn't appeal to the other. They bought a small handful of airplane legs in advance, but left travel dates unspecified. They identified some jobs for itinerants on each continent they planned to visit just in case Geoff couldn't sell any of his writing. They sold what they could of their belongings, amassing their meager budget for the year.

And then they took off.

At this writing, that was 25 years ago. Geoff has been a consultant since returning from the trip, with writing just one aspect of his profession rather than a blockbuster career in itself. But the better news, he and Martha married soon after their return and have spent the better part of that time raising four happy sons, now grown. What happened along the way – both on the trip and in the intervening period – are stories for another time. What we're most interested in for current purposes is the design of the experiments themselves.

When you are still living in the uncertain "if" phase, there are three actions you can take to simultaneously try to provoke a phase change to "when" and try to understand when you have entered that phase change. Some of these actions come naturally and will feel familiar to many readers who are unaware that they are natural provocateurs. The trick is to execute them with foresight purpose.

Situate. With a sense for how the future might unfold through different scenarios, actions that help situate you are ones in which you place bets that maximize the likelihood that your future desired state comes to pass. Without getting into scurrilous details of Geoff's early love life, he positioned himself through networking and his choices about social interactions to maximize the likelihood that he would cross paths with a woman whom he could spend his life with (or, some would say more accurately, one who was willing to put up with him for a lifetime).

Frame. Once you know what you are trying to achieve and are in a position to take action, you need to frame an experiment in a way that will give you data on whether a hypothesis is coming true and/or whether you can catalyze events in a way that will lead it to come true. The frame Geoff and Martha created around his writing was able to accomplish both: the trip was designed to give him sufficient free time and experience fodder to test whether he had it in him to focus, free up mind space, and treat writing as a career *and* to test whether they could cause a career in writing by allowing him to create a robust portfolio to jumpstart things.

Test. Testing is, of course, execution of the designed experiment. But the active work in this provocation goes beyond just pulling the trigger. It largely consists of constantly monitoring outcomes in a way that allows you to place new bets, frame further experiments, and launch new tests until you shift from "if" to "when." Sadly for Geoff's writing career, it became pretty apparent early on that he hated editing and would prefer going on a hike or sharing a beer after a long day on the road than focusing on putting pen to paper. No shortage of new experiments, with shifts from fiction to poetry to philosophy, or attempts at switching up writing windows and locations, could prevent the phase change to it just being a matter of when he would return to his job in consulting.

The key distinguishing feature of these three moves in the "if" phase is that you need to treat them as a system, interconnected and often executed repeatedly in a series. The "when" provocations on the other hand (as we will discuss in more detail in the next chapter) represent a discrete choice with mutually exclusive outcomes.

The depth of any step in the series will vary significantly, though. Sometimes, for example, positioning isn't needed because the actor is sufficiently confident that they don't need to hedge any bets and can instead move forward in one direction through a collection of tests. Other times, some period of stasis in a well-selected position can keep the actor under the radar from potential competitors long enough to create an advantage. We don't know for certain whether the protagonists in each of the following stories were purposely acting as provocateurs, but they have ended up as great examples of the moves in retrospect, regardless.

BETTING ON THE BUSINESS MODEL

In early 2008, four classmates at Wharton Business School, Neil Blumenthal, Andrew Hunt, David Gilboa, and Jeffrey Raider, wondered why prescription eyeglasses were not sold online. It's not that others hadn't had the same thought, but most believed such a business model was unsustainable. The eyewear market was characterized by a very small number of large global players controlling nearly all name-brand frames and distribution channels. Barriers to entry were high, to say the least. Additionally, the idea of buying eyewear online, a deeply tactile purchase, seemed doomed to fail in the earlier e-commerce days when buying books online made sense but – for example – personal fashion didn't. But there were signs that might change. Warby Parker was a provocateur in the shift from the separation of retail into "bricks and mortar" and "online" to "omnichannel."[1]

Ahead of many others who had likely explored the market, the four co-founders were able to both sense and demonstrate that high-touch retail experiences could effectively transfer online. As such, they were partially the cause of this moving from an "if" to a concrete "when." The convergence of two factors was key: the rapidly expanding e-commerce market and Americans' growing comfort with online shopping, and an eyewear industry with bloated "middle-man" costs that was ripe for disruption.

Against the backdrop of this landscape, Warby Parker launched a vertically integrated company that eliminated waste in the distribution system through a direct-to-consumer model, passing savings on to consumers. This, coupled with a deep passion for customer experience and a willingness to respond to feedback and iterate, has driven much of the success of this company – valued in late 2020 at a remarkable $3 billion. Not bad for a company whose name derives from the diaries of Jack Kerouac, a poster child for the hippie counterculture of the 1960s.

In the early days, the founders believed in the opportunity enough to go all-in in terms of the business model: positioning as a low-cost, online, convenient, and customer-obsessed alternative to larger competitors. But much of the company's continued success comes from a willingness to continually design, test, and reposition in response to the market. This has been ingrained in the DNA of the company right from inception. The bias to act and constantly adjust has lasted even after the business model has been proven successful and Warby Parker passed through the phase change.

Indeed, the series of moves they have made over time have an arc to the story familiar to any lovers of the "How I Built This" podcast from Guy Raz. Early feedback from classmates at Wharton about the importance of trying eyewear for fit and aesthetics led them to allow customers to try five pairs free. Early emails from first-adopter customers asking to visit a Warby Parker location to try on their glasses led co-founder Blumenthal to invite them to his home. Feedback gave the team confidence to expand into the brick-and-mortar space, first through pop-ups and shops within established retailers, and eventually to more than 125+ stores in operations across the United States and Canada. Although most of the company's sales are still online – that remains their primary business model – the retail stores signal Warby Parker's willingness to evolve in the face of market feedback. It also demonstrates how they tested and iterated on what a physical manifestation of their store would look like, including a traveling pop-up version using a retrofitted yellow school bus that arrived on the scene in 2016.

Warby Parker stands as an example of a company that used the "if" phase of uncertainty to its advantage both in the short term and long term. The bias to act through all three types of "if" provocation, alternating between test-and-learn and provoke-and-cause, is deeply engrained in the mindset and culture of the company. And as they have moved through the phase change, they have been able to even more directly drive (one of the "when" provocations that we will cover in more detail in the next chapter) the kinds of market shifts that continually keep them out in front of what had once been the incumbent players. From expanding into children's eyewear to launching a prescription app to building an augmented reality driven virtual try-on feature, they are (for now) the prime mover in the industry.

Warby Parker is just one model for moving through the "if" phase of building kinetic energy as the trend climbs to the top of the rollercoaster's peak. Sometimes you have the ability to keep up your forward momentum and relentlessly drive to the business model outcome you are confident in. Other times, more "active patience" is required, camping out on a beachhead position until it is time to forge ahead through the phase change.

USING A BEACHHEAD POSITION

Whether reading a "newspaper," monitoring your investment portfolio, keeping an eye on your front door while you're away, or engaging in any number of other mundane daily activities, chances are you are interacting with a subscription business model dozens of times per day. That subscription business model is more than likely enabled by a company called Zuora.[2]

Zuora was founded a long time ago, at least in start-up years, well before many of today's unicorns were glimmers in their founders' eyes. It was the 2007 brainchild of Tien Tzuo, who had a front-row seat to the accelerated adoption of subscription models as the Chief Strategy Officer of Salesforce.com, a company built on the idea of software-as-a-service. Tzuo called early on that, as companies sought to focus more on customer satisfaction, they would shift from being manufacturing-centric to being service-centric. And they would need a billing system that was different from traditional enterprise resource planning (ERP) systems to enable that shift.

Along with two other executives that he brought on from Webex, Tzuo set off to create the e-commerce solution that would provide the backbone for companies he anticipated rushing into the space. From the beginning, he recognized that he ran the risk of having the much larger, much-better-funded ERP providers attempting to pigeonhole Zuora as a one-dimensional solution focused only on, for example, billing. He launched a long-term campaign both to popularize the subscription economy and to make sure that Zuora stood to benefit from providing the full range of services required by companies operating with that business model.

Over time, Tzuo emerged as a prime example of a company that – convinced of the coming eventuality of subscriptions as a dominant model – worked the position provocation relentlessly. Ahead of the curve of large companies using subscriptions on a wide basis, Zuora bided its time with smaller companies in the early years, optimizing the way it created value beyond providing the guts of a billing system. One benefit of working with start-ups was that it allowed Zuora to see unmet customer needs in much starker relief: early-stage companies rarely have the luxury of focusing on anything but their core competence.

A recent perusal of Zuora's site reveals a slew of services it has been able to bring to customers:

- "Enabled [company name omitted] to integrate all its mobility services onto one platform for a seamless customer experience."

- "Allowed [company name omitted] to quickly build new functionality that integrates with their platforms and processes for improved billing, reporting, pricing, and packaging."

- "Gave [company name omitted] flexible and scalable pricing and packaging, customer insights and financial reporting to better understand their customers and the business."

It also reveals that it has ridden the phase change effectively. With the explosive rise of subscription models across a wide range of sectors, Zuora now is positioned to help much larger companies like Schneider Electric and NCR.

But this didn't happen by accident. From the early days of Zuora, Tzuo was a thought leader on the subscription economy. He engaged with journalists on his views of the changed revenue model and software-as-a-service (SaaS) generally, prolifically blogging in *Subscribed Weekly* in an attempt to bring about the phase change that paid off his position even more rapidly. The company also runs *Subscribed* magazine, the *Subscribed* podcast, and has offered Subscribed Awards. In 2018, Tzuo published a business strategy book about the subscription economy, *Subscribed: Why the Subscription Model Will Be Your Company's Future – and What to Do About It*.

Through the company's involvement, Wall Street analysts have changed the way they value and analyze SaaS business models, shifting away from measures such as P/E ratios in favor of ones like reoccurring profit margins, retention rate, and a "growth efficiency index." Tzuo and Zuora have been major provocateurs for – and beneficiaries of – the phase change that brought all-things-as-a-service to the mainstream.

There are many other examples of individuals and companies who have effectively used patience with the position provocation as a way to create long-term advantage. Although the specifics depend on how much one believes about various versions of the creation story of Amazon, it's not hard to argue that Jeff Bezos saw early on that a beachhead position in books would allow him to build out his business model and experience in a way that would make it an inevitability that he would one day become the world's wealthiest individual and his company, a retail juggernaut the likes of which the world had never seen.[3]

One of our favorite examples of this type of provocation, though, comes from the world of academia. Rosalind Picard is an MIT professor and founder and director of the Affective Computing Research Group at the MIT Media Lab. Professor Picard essentially founded an entire branch of computer science that allows artificial intelligence systems to infer emotion from human expressions. Although this technology is well through the phase change at this point – used by industries from ad agencies to car manufacturers – in the mid- to late 1990s there was still a serious question of "if" it would ever catch on.

Picard has shared stories with colleagues of ours about a conscious choice she made at the time to focus on building her profile as a science-based researcher before pushing too hard on the idea that there was any connection between computers and emotion. Emotion was not considered a serious topic within the male-dominated world of computer science at the time. Picard redirected their attention to her chops as an expert in signal processing until she had confidence that she would not be seen as "the emotion lady." In other words, she acted to provoke an attractive future for herself by honing a position from which she could – in time – make small moves to encourage affective computing to take off. Today, it is projected to grow to a $140 billion industry by 2025, largely because one woman 25 years ago acted, but with patience.[4]

These stories have involved a protagonist who was either reasonably confident in an overall business model and opportunity (Warby Parker, Zuora, Amazon) or had the foresight to recognize the importance of not trying to rush outcomes before some preconditions were in place (Professor Picard). Sometimes, though, there is a sufficiently intertwined tangle of uncertainties on the path forward that the only choice you have is to act one step at a time, inspired largely by a deep-seated principle about the right direction forward.

UNTANGLING MULTIPLE VECTORS OF UNCERTAINTY

The famed success of restaurateur Danny Meyer and his Shake Shack empire might look today like it just stumbled upon the inevitable shift from fast food to "fine casual." When it was founded in 2001, though, that trend was anything but inevitable. It took Meyer's exploration of the business model from multiple different angles to at least partially cause the phase change. But Meyer knew early on that he wanted to "Stand For Something Good."

The original conception for Shake Shack bears little resemblance to what it has become today. It started life as a small hot dog stand in New York City whose purpose was more about deepening the community of the Madison Square Park neighborhood (close to where he had two restaurants at the time, neither of which remain in his portfolio: Eleven Madison Park and Tabla) than it was about creating a global phenomenon. Had Meyer known what was possible at the time, he might have been exploring multiple different uncertainties simultaneously: Is it possible to sell what has historically been considered fast food using premium ingredients? Is it possible to align business interests with community interests? Is it possible to position on simplicity and a signature strength, rather than trying to satisfy diverse customers in different ways?

Sometimes, though, the best way to act in the uncertain "if" phase – even if you have envisioned scenarios for the future effectively – is not to try to solve for the whole all at once. Instead, act in line with a core ethos and take small steps until the future better reveals itself. Meyer started with a focus on the neighborhood and found ways to support local workers, including off-season coat-check staff at his other restaurants.

He donated a percentage of any profits to Madison Square Park, letting his focus on creating great experiences lead him to his next adventure.[5] He cast aside the long-held belief that fast food must be focused on quick turnaround and instead illustrated that people care about quality ingredients and a friendly customer experience. Perhaps most counterintuitively, at least considering the norm today to be (or at least claim to be) obsessed with customers, he focused first inward:

> At the center of Shake Shack's mission is Danny Meyer's philosophy of "enlightened hospitality." In essence, it's a set of priorities: the idea is to create a welcoming atmosphere first for employees, next for customers, and then for the outside community, suppliers, and, finally, investors . . . Shake Shack's vision is to Stand For Something Good in all aspects of its business, including the exceptional team it hires and trains, the premium ingredients making up the menu, the community engagement, and the design of the Shacks. Stand For Something Good is a call to action to all stakeholders—the team, guests, communities, suppliers and investors—and it actively invites them all to share in this philosophy.[6]

At this writing, Shake Shack has close to 300 locations globally and while the pandemic has thrown all short-term planning out the window, it looks as though it has lived the phase change, perhaps not in a way that Danny Meyer had always envisioned but in a way consistent with his ideals. And judging by one of his more recent quotes, it appears he is not acting under the presumption of not "if" the model will succeed, stating: "We've reached a critical mass where there's just no going back. And I think that's awesome."[7]

Although we may not recognize it as such, we all live with the onslaught of thousands of provocateurs every day who position (sometimes largely based on principle, or brand) and then run a series of framing and testing exercises to see what will stick: anyone and everyone on social media. Admittedly, there are some social dabblers who are only online to post a random vacation photo and then never look at the "like" rate. But the vast majority of social posts are from people who are trying to read the response signal for when they have hit upon something that could make it mainstream. From TikTokkers to up-and-coming influencers, we're surrounded by them, and by "them," we mean us.

It does make one wonder why, then, the impulse to act and watch for a response seems automatic and even addictive in the realm of social media, but then when we put the screens away and return to the offline world, we seem to subdue or even suppress that instinct. Is it because we are not hiding being a tiny little screen of anonymity (which, ironically, is a false sense of security since digital social media often achieves the opposite effect)? Is it because we are switching out of our personal lives and into our professional lives? Is it because we can sense a lurking mass of supporters who have our back and will come out in droves if we can get that post *just right*? It's almost certainly all these things and more, many rooted in the fatal flaws that we discussed in Part I.

We all have the power to be provocateurs – no matter our title or perceived position relative to others or age or experience. It is easy to imagine that it is only the domain of the Musks and the AOCs and the Bransons, given how their actions are celebrated (or vilified) in the press. But if we leave it to only them, we are relying too much on the randomness of their moves being right to carry us forward in the face of uncertainty. Provocation needs to be everyone's job if it is going to unlock scaled forward momentum to overcome organizational, governmental, and societal inertia.

Several years ago, we had a new undergraduate analyst join our firm who was – or appeared to be – a rabid Fantasy Football fan. She immediately jumped into almost any league she could find at work: in her local office, on her project teams, and in her practice area (i.e., the community of specialists she had joined). And she was pretty good.

One of her keys to success seemed to be that she had a license, extended from her time at university, to a platform that enabled large-scale analysis and visualization of publicly available data to understand trending topics and – importantly – how those topics interrelated with one another. She seemed to have honed the art of aiming that platform every week at the world's conversations about fantasy player moves (trades, adds, drops, and so on), and she used that to move faster than her opponents in tweaking her weekly line-up. It turns out that's not all she was up to, though, as she told us recently.

She had joined a part of our consulting practice that uses, as part of its business model, a variety of methods to better understand unspoken (rather than self-reported) market and customer needs. As a data analytics major in college, she had become fascinated with the power of gaining even a tiny temporal edge over others by using large-scale, real-time data sets. And she also discovered that talking about her passion in social settings ran dry with many people pretty quickly. As a result, she played around with some ways to help others better understand why she was so excited about this field. Some of them worked, some failed utterly, but that is how she discovered the world of fantasy football. It was something others wanted to talk about.

Fast forward to when she joined Deloitte, and she naturally assumed that she would find a whole community of similarly minded data fanatics in her practice and that everyone had access to the platform she had been playing around with in college.

Hardly anyone had heard of it.

And even worse, when she brought it up as a tool that might be used in project work through different levels of management, she was met largely with skepticism: it sounded similar to other tools the firm had used before; she was just an undergrad analyst and couldn't possibly understand the level of rigor required in our work. It looked just a bit too pretty in its outputs to be helpful. Objection piled on dismissive objection.

Most readers can probably guess how this all played out. She provoked. She put herself in a position to gain the attention of others in her communities related to topics of shared interest. Some paid attention and some didn't, but with those that did, she framed a series of tests to see what garnered the most attention to the software she was so excited about. Ultimately, she triggered a phase change when one of the practice leaders got exposed to her fantasy prowess and wondered "what would happen if we used this tool on this project I've got going . . ."

As with the lead story in this chapter, slightly apocryphal, yes. These stories abound, though, and we're pretty sure that as we start to pay more attention to the actions of those around us we'll discover that many have it in themselves to provoke the future they want whether they know they are doing it or not. After all, if Geoff's little brothers could provoke a reaction from him almost as soon as they learned to walk, we're pretty sure that we all have it in us to poke just a little more and DO SOMETHING!

The whole purpose of the "if" phase of provocations is to put your organization in a better position to see when the "if" might become a "when." Whether it's Warby Parker doing so by consistently tinkering, or Shake Shack by iterating while remaining true to core principles, or Geoff himself on his world wanders, the idea is to simultaneously be the cause of change and to better get ready for it. In most walks of life, we don't believe there is such a thing as perpetual uncertainty. Most everything resolves at some point; it just may take longer than we anticipated, or it may break in a direction that we don't like.

The rare exceptions often have to do with more metaphysical or epistemological matters. It is unlikely that we will ever be able to provoke a resolution to questions like, "What does it mean to know?" or "What constitutes the barrier between existence and nonexistence?" Thankfully, these are not the types of questions that most of us need to face most of the time in our day-to-day lives. However, we would love to hear any and all ideas on tests that could be framed to trigger a move beyond uncertainty around these questions.

The phase change doesn't show itself in a moment of enlightenment. In fact, if you "know" that it is happening, then you have probably waited too long to shift into the "when" mode of provocation. The acceptance of the phase change is likely going to require some degree of cognitive dissonance to overcome the fatal flaws discussed in Part I. It is easy to look back on the history of others stumbling in the face of false positives (Google Glass?) and false negatives ($75-a-barrel oil price and climbing in mid-2018).

But that's the point: to enter the phase change effectively and in a timely enough way to gain advantage, it's critical not to use historical guideposts. Instead, provoke to the point of confidence in the "if" phase of uncertainty, and then act with the conviction of "when." There's no guarantee that you're going to get it right, but there's a higher likelihood of getting most things right in the face of increasing uncertainty if you can tamp down the instinct to go collect more data. Just go DO SOMETHING!

CHAPTER 8

Drive and Adapt:
Taking Control

For a couple of guys who spend a lot of time together and who think very similarly, we have wildly different tastes. Steve likes to listen to instrumental jazz; Geoff is obsessed with live jam band music. Sidle up to a bar with us and Geoff will likely have an IPA in hand or a glass of whatever gin's lying around (ice optional); Steve prefers a finely crafted bourbon cocktail. So it comes as no surprise that we discovered another stark difference when we were discussing times when we each had to literally force our bodies to go do something while every instinct said, "Don't do it!"

When Geoff first heard about Gym Jones from Steve, he was pretty sure they were talking about a cult leader who precipitated a sequence of terrible events in a South American jungle in the late 1970s. Turns out, in fact, that the modern incarnation is even more terrifying to some: a private collaborative of ultra-fit trainers and training houses around the world who take on only those willing to work hard – and suffer – as their belief is that there are no shortcuts to physical fitness. Famous athletes, secretive military operatives, and sculpted movie stars have made the cut in the past. So has Steve, Geoff discovered.

The story came up because we were wrestling with what a "when" provocation would feel like if brought to life in the physical world. What does it feel like to overcome extreme cognitive dissonance to force your body to do something it doesn't want to? Steve's experience was in testing for one of the Gym Jones certifications. Here's how he described it:

> When I did the Gym Jones certification, it was led by Bobby Maximus – a former UFC fighter and one of Men's Health's Top 100 Fittest People Ever.[1] He emphasized the power of the mind in training, so they put you through some real psychological tests. One of the tests they give you is to do a 60-second, all-out, sprint on the Airdyne bike (one of those old-school "fan" bikes). When I say all-out, I mean, all-out. The goal is to "score" as many calories burned as possible. Here's the twist though: you're competing with the 16 other people in the certification session and the top 8 in calories get to be done for the day. The bottom 8 have to do another all-out sprint. And the process repeats. Then 4, then 2, then 1. If anyone's ever done anything truly all-out, one is sufficient for the day. You definitely don't want to have to do this more than once, let alone 3–4 times. There's nothing worse than a 60-second sprint. It's different than 20 seconds (you can do anything for 20 seconds); it starts to really hurt after about 20 because you get lactic acid building up in your legs. To get a good score, you just have to turn off your mind, which is telling you to stop so the pain will go away. You have to tell yourself it will be fine. If you try to do an 80% effort for 60 seconds, you'll definitely have to do it again. And the worst result is that you have to do this again . . . and again. Bobby has since become a friend and I know this is one of his favorite mind-*you-know-whats*. The fact that I was 41 and probably, on average, 10 years older than others in

the room – no discount. The fact that all the others were professional trainers and I was a businessperson who spent 300k miles in the air every year – no discount. You just had to completely surrender to go all out and deal with it and know the pain would come. I knew I wouldn't come first, but I also knew that some people who were fitter perhaps wouldn't commit fully, so I set my goal to come at least eighth. Believe it or not, I came in exactly that place and set a personal calorie record in the process. And then I lay down and curled up for a while and enjoyed watching the bottom eight rinse and repeat.

Likely proving Steve's maxim wrong, Geoff wouldn't have lasted 20 seconds. Instead, his story came from a very different place and domain of adrenaline-seeking: bungee jumping. He would be hard-pressed to say that he loves – or even likes – the activity. He's done it a sum total of twice: once on the aforementioned, long-ago wander around the world, and once on a family trip to celebrate a certain birthday of Martha's mother.

This was several years ago when the extended clan made a trek to southern Africa, to enjoy some family time. But the "kids" – Geoff's four teenaged sons and their five cousins – were looking for even more adventure. Somehow, they settled on bungee-jumping despite Geoff's protestations; even after two and a half decades, he still remembered launching himself from the Pipeline bridge in Queenstown, New Zealand . . . the massive cranial pressure and sheer terror completely unabated by the two shots of courage he and Martha had taken beforehand. But as any reader with them will know, kids have a funny persuasive power.

Geoff found himself walking out to the center of a span of bridge in Zimbabwe, knowing with perfect certainty that he did not feel like going through with this. With each step, he was assailed with data and reasons not to carry through: "The safety of this equipment is totally unknown! I already have a bit of a backache and who knows what this might do to that! If I do it, I'm going to get roped into buying the damn pictures afterwards! I'm a grown man and have nothing to prove to any of these people!" And then he strapped in and jumped.

Though he might like to paint it otherwise, this was not a moment of heroic bravery. If anything, it was a willful, non-pharmaceutical firing of his GABA receptors – self-induced and temporary – and to this day he can't explain the rational reason for having acted the way he did. However, in retrospect he was happy he did, as was Steve when he was able to uncurl himself from the gym floor.

This is the mindset that we're trying to encourage in any provocateur as they pass through the phase change: to act even in the face of doubt and/or incomplete data, not hesitating too much but not being foolhardy, either. As optimists, we're hopeful that everyone has it in themselves to act this way. Abstracted or out

of the moment, it's easy to say, "Well I would never do that." In fact, after we swapped stories, we both concluded that no amount of coercion or motivation could have gotten each of us to take the action of the other. But the stories in this chapter give us hope that the will to go out and DO SOMETHING! lies in all of us.

As soon as you have clarity that you are entering a phase change, *how* you provoke needs to shift to reflect the reality of the shift from "if" to "when." But that doesn't mean that all "when" provocations are the same. The two dimensions that will help determine the nature of the appropriate action are (1) the degree to which we believe we can shape the desired outcome and (2) the complexity of the pathway to the desired outcome.

As we set about exploring the ideas for *Provoke*, we found we were stumbling across lots of examples of companies and individuals who made a brilliant strategic move, but one that appeared to be missing some degree of intentionality. Perhaps the old adage is true – it is better to be lucky than good. But the best provocateurs – as the subsequent stories will bring to life – bring a combination of foresight, well-timed action, and a constant attention to "what's next" in the market to constantly work the swirl between catalyzing the world they envision and riding the waves that they make.

DRIVE

Of any of the provocations, Drive is probably the one most often pictured when one thinks about directly impacting one's own destiny. Simply put, drive is when a single organization can have a meaningful impact on the outcome of a broader trend, where an actor has the opportunity to "just do it."

Often, if you catch a trend early enough in the phase change, you may have a slightly higher ability to influence the outcome, although we have observed it's increasingly rare that any single organization has enough influence to truly go it alone. But Drive is also the move that requires the most confidence and commitment to seeing it through, even in the face of plenty of evidence that the move is anything but a sure thing.

One of our favorite stories of this type of provocation comes from the early days of the automobile. In the early 1900s, William "Billy" Durant owned and ran the largest horse-drawn carriage company in the United States: the Durant-Dort Carriage Company. And he hated cars. Not just because they were a newfangled threat to his business, but because he – like many of the day – thought they were dangerous and noisy. He even went to far as to forbid his daughter from riding in them.[2]

Given the focus on safety and emissions standards in today's world, it's hard to imagine what the advent of the automobile looked like and felt like. It would not be dissimilar to autonomous vehicles being unleashed on the streets of 2021 with few operating standards in place and complete lack of transparency regarding ownership, operation, and accountability. In two summer months in Detroit in 1908, 31 people were killed in car crashes, and so many were injured it went unrecorded. The reports from on the ground at the time makes it unsurprising that some saw the automobile as a machine of pure evil:

> There were no stop signs, warning signs, traffic lights, traffic cops, driver's education, lane lines, street lighting, brake lights, driver's licenses or posted speed limits. Our current method of making a left turn was not known, and drinking-and-driving was not considered a serious crime. Streetcars, which

ran up the center of the streets, were becoming the most dangerous place in the city for pedestrians. Disembarking streetcar riders had to run a gauntlet of racing cars, trucks, motorcycles, and horse-drawn buggies to cross the street safely. Pedestrians often could not judge how close a fast-approaching car was to them and scrambled like squirrels to get out of the way. The most appalling tragedies were the number of children struck and killed by autos as they played in the street, many times in front of their own homes. In the 1920s, 60% of automobile fatalities nationwide were children under age 9.[3]

Despite this mayhem, Durant recognized an opportunity. Beyond the insight that automobiles were here to stay (helped by a begrudging admission that he had enjoyed a ride in an early Buick), he recognized that the barrier to success of the industry lay as much or more in the supply side of the system as it did in the uptake of demand or the ability to create safer operating conditions.

The industry was highly fragmented, with over 45 car companies operating in the United States, the majority selling only a small number of cars each year and frequently going out of business before delivery. Safety and manufacturing standards were nonexistent. Durant believed that if he could consolidate the largest and most reliable manufacturers, he could produce a more standardized, reliable product and drive the weaker auto companies out of business. This in turn could create a virtuous cycle that ultimately would increase consumer confidence and speed automobile adoption. General Motors was born, pioneering both the automobile holding company and the vertically integrated automobile company as Durant rolled up the Buick, Oldsmobile, Oakland, Cadillac, and other brands.[4]

Durant's tale can also serve as a cautionary one, though. Over the course of the following decade he lost control of GM, regained it, and lost it a second time. Durant was constantly out a bit over his skis when it came to creditors' patience. However, the underlying result of Durant's vision has persisted in some form for over 100 years. At its peak GM had a 50% market share in the United States, and it was the world's largest automaker from 1931 through 2007.

Over a century after Billy Durant changed the face of automobiles, another provocateur with an inclination to drive toward the future did the same in the field of communication. Pony Ma maintains a considerably lower profile than did the supersalesman Durant, but what he has accomplished with TenCent and WeChat is arguably on its way to having an even bigger impact on society.

Ma Huateng (aka Pony Ma) was in the ideal place at the ideal time, living through China's rapid rise from an agrarian society to an industrial powerhouse that became the world's factory in just less than 40 years. Ma witnessed this transformation firsthand, recognizing how quickly society and people within it will adapt and adopt new ways of doing things that clearly make their lives better. Today, regardless of where we are in the world and our socioeconomic class, we spend much of our lives on (and enabled by) our smartphones. But that clearly has not always been the case.[5]

The phase changes that Ma recognized in or around 2010 – and positioned himself and his company to take massive advantage of – were the rise of the smartphone as the primary mechanism for accessing the Internet and the subsequent shift to instant messaging as a way to stay in touch. How much since then in the TenCent and WeChat story is cause rather than effect can be debated, but there's no doubt that the company helped lead the way as a key catalyst in the exponential rise of smartphone use. And since then, it has always seemed to be able to stay one step ahead of the next trend. WeChat has continuously added to its wealth of offerings to lock its large, loyal user base into the ecosystem. As of 2020, the range of WeChat services includes the offerings of multiple large-tech companies in the West, including Google, Uber, SnapChat, Amazon, Craigslist, and Facebook.[6]

Many of these offerings achieved great success due to the company's understanding of the needs of its customer base and partners, and a recognition of a whitespace in the market. A prime example of this is WeChat's "Red Packets" offering. Introduced in 2014 on their WeChat Pay digital wallet, Red Packets was an offer they used to drive heavy platform traffic by redefining the Chinese red gift envelopes, or *hongbao*, a key tradition on Chinese New Year. It was a strategic move that offered a more seamless and virtual method for its users to continue the tradition, with interactive and fun elements added to the customer experience. For example, "WeChat users could allocate a sum of money that would be distributed among a specified group of friends on a 'first come, first served' basis. Thus, people would frequently check their WeChat app so as not to miss out on the gift. This feature proved to be very popular as people would compete to get the best red envelopes, and the thrill of winning or losing led to more and more envelopes being sent." In just one year, between 2015 and 2016, the number of red envelopes being sent exploded eightfold to over 8 billion, an exponential spike that would get any adherent to the strategic value of platforms salivating.[7]

Look hard enough and you'll likely find a great drive story at the advent of any successful industry shift. That was certainly true of one of the first blockbuster medical device products: the drug-eluting stent. In the early 1990s, one of the weekly vascular surgery conferences at the University of British Columbia (UBC) found itself short of a speaker. With no established researchers or doctors available, the speaking spot was filled at the last minute by a medical student at UBC, Bill Hunter. As Hunter presented his summer research regarding the use of paclitaxel and other agents to target inflammation in rheumatoid arthritis, in the audience, Lindsay Machan, M.D., had a eureka moment.[8]

Coming into the conference, Machan and the rest of his profession were carrying with them a vexing treatment challenge that had arisen with the increased use of stents: tube-shaped devices placed within coronary arteries to keep them open while treating coronary heart disease. The challenge had to do with "restenosis" – a condition when part of an artery with a stent gets blocked – which doctors were observing had an incidence rate of between 15% and 30% for these procedures. As Machan sat in the audience that day at UBC, it occurred to him that the research Hunter was presenting might have a different application. Paclitaxel might also be successful in reducing restenosis if delivered through stents. He knew already that the problem of restenosis had likely triggered a phase change to a new stenting technology becoming inevitable. The question was *which* technology. Shortly after the conference, Machan, Hunter, and another colleague co-founded Angiotech to answer that question.[9]

The team at Angiotech invented the industry's first drug-eluting stent and the company's initial lead product, TAXUS®, subsequently licensed to Boston Scientific, has been implanted in over five million patients.[10] The company's incredible success was built on the founders seeing a clear problem and opportunity – and an efficacious solution through which they could be first to market to reap rewards. From a business strategy perspective, there was little complexity here; fueled by their own research and trials, as well as similar medical breakthroughs globally, the founders knew which direction they needed to drive Angiotech and they created the future they desired for the company.

It is perhaps easy to think of all drive stories as heroic journeys in which a single actor has a brilliant insight and uses that to create his or her desired future. But look a little closer at all three of the stories and you'll find other characters lurking in the wings with a touch of circumstantial chemistry to boot. Neither Hunter nor Machan would likely have been able to envision – let alone create – Angiotech had they not collided at the fateful UBS conference. Billy Durant's interest in the automobile business model was snapped into attention by a rival carriage-maker who had bought the fledgling Buick Company and was frustrated by its cost structure. And Pony Ma had Zhang Xiaolong, also known as Allen Zhang, who brought him the idea of an instant messenger app in 2010, inspired in part by an app from the West. All had a trusted advisor of sorts, perhaps suggesting that the provocateurs with the keenest foresight for spotting a phase change have the keenest listening and observational skills as well.

ADAPT

The act of adapting to a foregone conclusion that doesn't favor you is the hardest provocation of all. Sometimes, that's due to operational or positioning challenges. But more often the biggest challenges are emotional ones, because by definition this reality is one in which you have little ability to shape a future that is advantageous to you, and a great degree of complexity in the path forward. It therefore requires an admission that your business model is no longer fit for purpose. Charged with all the biases outlined in Part I and amplified by concerns about legacy and respect for the past, it often can feel nearly impossible to declare "enough's enough."

We discussed earlier in the book the distant cousin of the pop-up firm, the *wind-down* firm. This is a version of the adapt provocation that typically befalls companies that either didn't envision well or didn't move fast enough as they exited the phase change: essentially, they are left no choice but to wind down as they see the wrecking ball swing toward them. It is usually far better – for customers and for executive psyches – to feel as though they are able to adapt on their own, better terms. Sometimes this means extending the going-concern life of the company. Other times, it means substantially reconfiguring assets and business models to play in the market in a different way, aiming for a new future desired outcome.

Consider some of the energy companies alluded to in Chapter 6, Envision. Some will end up overhauling their business models such that what was once an oil-and-gas supermajor may end up being a diversified energy provider leveraging primarily renewable sources, out of carbon-extractive assets for good; others will recognize that the best thing they can do for shareholders is to drive down their operational costs and ride the carbon curve until its end. Still others will break themselves up and sell their assets to the highest bidder as soon as feasible.

Clearly, while it's great to be able to see the wrecking ball coming, it's even better when you can get out of the way and configure yourself to take advantage of the emerging trend. This requires embedding – with foresight – a plan to adapt predictably, building it into your business model from the outset. It's quite challenging, however, to take a well-established, well-loved company to a different place even while others may be pressuring significantly in the other direction, because they do not yet see the phase change that you do.

Intel has, for many decades, been one of those well-established, well-loved companies. Many interpret its name as literally the "inside" guts of what makes computers work. Founded by Gordon Moore (perhaps ironically the person who popularized the notion of exponential change, which is at the heart of so much disruptive opportunity these days) in 1968, Intel is one of the original Silicon Valley residents. The company released the first commercially available dynamic random-access memory (DRAM) in 1970, which quickly became the bestselling memory chip in the world. But by the early 1980s, Intel's DRAM business faced significant competitive pressure from low-cost semiconductor manufacturers in Japan.

At about that time, Intel COO Andy Grove posed a question to Moore, the company's chairman and CEO: "If we got kicked out and the board brought in a new CEO, what do you think he would do?"[11]

Although Grove may have intended the question as rhetorical, it wasn't much of a stretch to see it as fundamental, as Intel moved from the possibility of being commoditized to the probability of being commoditized. Intel had become simply unable to compete with lower cost suppliers in Japan that were willing and able to undercut prices to take share from Intel. The question was not if competition would render Intel completely obsolete, it was a matter of how long they could hold on against the inevitable; it was simply a matter of "when."

Moore's answer, freed from the reality that he was in fact the one with the ability to make such a decision, reflected this painful truth: "He would get us out of memories."

We hypothesize that this conversation is not a unique occurrence in the C-suite of businesses experiencing the threat of crippling disruption. The focus on quarterly results mandated by Wall Street ensures that leaders are highly attuned to anything that might knock them off track. Too many of them, however, fail to realize that the war is over – the question is not if their business will atrophy (in which case, it would be perfectly reasonable to continue the fight) but by how much, and will it fail? Many leaders' experience as longtime company insiders prevents them from seeing that the hypothetical idea of adapting to a new reality – to turn away from the model that had been at the heart of their careers to date – is more an imperative than an option.

Andy Grove was nothing if not an insider at Intel. He became Intel's third employee after escaping Communist-controlled Hungary and moving to the United States at the age of 20. He had been at Moore's side during Intel's meteoric rise. His response, though, was almost the antithesis of what you would expect from a lifer. He suggested they take the business they had spent decades building from nothing, and essentially surrender it to their competition to adapt: "Why shouldn't you and I walk out the door, come back and do it ourselves?"[12]

There is perhaps an alternative reality in which Gordon Moore takes Grove's suggestion as black humor. Perhaps Grove reconsiders his provocation after such a reaction, and the two have a good laugh before getting back to thinking about how to beat their Japanese semiconductor rivals. In that world, Intel very likely no longer exists except as perhaps a business school case study on how lower cost producers can disrupt a dominant industry incumbent – replacing Clayton Christensen's example of how the mini-mill disrupted the steel industry.

Luckily for Intel, Andy Grove and Gordon Moore are true provocateurs. They realized that to not adapt was to concede Intel's fate. Then they went about undertaking the work of getting Intel out of the business in which they made their name and into their business of the future: microprocessors. The process wasn't an easy or immediate one. In 1986 Intel lost $173 million and was forced to enact layoffs, plant closings, and other cutbacks to facilitate their adaption. But by carrying through with his move to adapt, Grove (who succeeded Moore as CEO in 1987) positioned Intel as the primary hardware supplier to the rapidly growing PC industry, leading to a market capitalization at the time of this writing of close to a quarter of a trillion dollars.

As 2020 unfolded, the COVID pandemic forced everyone to consider a little more deeply their assumptions about what in their life was stable and what was not. Physical and financial health, employment, free movement, and "something to look forward to" all of a sudden seemed a lot more tenuous to a lot more people than had previously been the case. Full industries were not immune. There have been remarkable stories of adaptation to emerge from those times, but many of them were presumed at the time to be temporary. Retrofitting production lines to switch from car assembly to ventilator assembly or turning local restaurants into collection and distribution centers certainly took bravery in the face of traditional notions of high performance, but they often weren't framed as "forever moves."

The energy industry, though, has needed to consider forever moves throughout almost every aspect of its value system since the advent of the energy transition. Despite assurances that the industry has lived through energy transitions before and they'll do so again, there's a strong argument that we have never lived through a real energy transition – that is, the systemic overhauling of the vast majority of the existing world's infrastructure to make way for a new, cleaner one. Most of what we have lived through can be better characterized instead as energy additions. Many executives in the industry have reacted as one might have expected Moore and Grove to in the early 1980s: to batten down the hatches and get creative in order to figure out how to protect a proven moneymaker. Thankfully, there is a small and growing handful who demonstrate the bias to adapt.

We recently were struck by the comments of one CEO of a player in the U.S. energy space, not necessarily just for the changes she was seeking to enact, but for the mindset she was bringing to her organization. Here's what Paula Gold-Williams of CPS Energy, an electric utility in Texas, had to say in late 2019:

> At CPS Energy, we are evolving. However, I want our company to always be hungry to do better and improve operations in a way that is proactive and anticipatory. We need to continually see how we can do the Wayne Gretzky. How do we increasingly anticipate where the energy puck is going to go? We cannot continue to be comfortable in reactive mode, even if we are good at it . . . We must improve our ability to anticipate where and how both customer preferences and the energy industry are growing. I want our utility and all of our employees to get used to that. Now the challenge is that we also have to get and stay comfortable with ambiguity. That continues to be rather contrary to our industry's historical foundation. Since we are comprised, in part, by a bunch of engineers, analysts, and accountants, we primarily prefer to structure most everything. As an example, accountants, like myself, want everything to be in balance. There have to be rules. We always need our debits to equal our credits. I now often ask, what if this industry

needs something that we can't quite imagine? Trying to think that everything's going to be perfect, linear, and in balance, is not realistic. We must fight our inclination to avoid uncertainty, realizing we cannot stop change. The inertia of evolution will occur, whether we are ready or not. So, I stress at CPS Energy that we must embrace ambiguity. The world functions in degrees of grey, not just black and white. I believe that the grey should set us free. It eliminates the feeling and perception of confinement.[13]

Some have told us that the willingness to adapt equates to a willingness to capitulate. Or that adhering to the notion of the scaled equivalent of a pop-up firm is akin to giving up. We take great solace from the obvious reality that Gold-Williams' mindset sounds like the furthest away from giving up.

Distilled from these stories, one could conclude that the drive and adapt provocations require acting with purpose at the right time and in the right context. Indeed, it would suggest that as you enter the phase change, the "safe" option of letting others go first in favor of a fast follower strategy is not really safe at all. In the old days of linear change and the primacy of analysis anchored in lessons from the past, that might have worked. But we're finding that, increasingly, nothing beats a move to just DO SOMETHING! to catalyze the future that works for you and what you want to achieve.

CHAPTER 9

Activate: Harnessing Your Ecosystem

Although ridiculous both as an example and as a fad, the "Wave" in sports stadiums pretty well encapsulates the idea of how to spur collective action – the idea at the heart of the activate provocation. For any reader not familiar with this curious social trend, it entails one person – or a small group of people – spontaneously standing up in the middle of a huge audience, throwing their hands in the air and yodel-shouting some sort of noise. If it goes well, their neighbors catch on and do the same, with a knock-on effect to other neighbors down the line until the controller of the jumbotron sees what's happening and trains the camera on the activity. At this point the movement can take on a life of its own, gradually enveloping the entire stadium audience in a rolling "wave" that circles in an accelerating style until it collapses under its own weight.

That's when it goes well.

When it goes badly, the aspiring provocateur is left standing with his arms in the air as he turns beet red and whimpers out a few feeble "Who's with me's" before sitting down in shame to drown his sorrows.

Thankfully whether we are talking about Activating social movements or spurring economic growth, it rarely requires exposing yourself to the boos and laughs of tens of thousands of spectators.

The Activate provocation involves working with and through an ecosystem to get things done. It's unique from the others, however, because while the provocateur may see a very straightforward path to their desired outcome, they have little ability to directly influence – except at the very outset – whether it is achieved. At its heart, it is a move to trigger a knock-on effect that, once set in motion, you just have to hope is seen all the way through. Sometimes, it is a well-planned and well-executed series of predictable knock-on effects that you can set off to your advantage – not unlike the triple bank shot of a pool shark. Other times, the provocateur can't quite see the series of events that will lead to their desired outcome and instead needs to send out a signal to others and hope for the best, monitoring and signaling further as the future unfolds with greater clarity.

One story, which includes a blend of direct activation and signaling, comes from the civic space: the story of a city that at one point appeared destined to enter a phase change to inevitable decline and stagnation until a collaboration of different types of institutions banded together to activate a different type of future.

First settled by the French in 1754 as the site of Fort Duquesne, Pittsburgh, Pennsylvania was captured by the British in 1758 and functioned as the gateway to the Ohio River Valley frontier during the eighteenth and nineteenth centuries. By the early 1900s, Pittsburgh had grown into a dominant force in the production of the coal and steel inputs that fueled America's industrial might. Forty percent of the nation's coal came from within 100 miles of Pittsburgh in surrounding Allegheny County. Based in the city, by the 1920s U.S. Steel was the world's largest steel producer and first billion-dollar corporation; Pittsburgh produced one third of the national output of both finished and rolled steel. For many years, the city was a great example of what Michael Porter calls a "cluster," with natural competitive advantages that extended to other, related industries, including electrical machinery, railroad cars, tin plate, glass, fire brick, and aluminum finishing.[1]

But by the 1980s, Pittsburgh and the Rust Belt more broadly had entered a period of significant decline as deregulation hit and lower-cost foreign competitors made significant market gains into the U.S. market. Many cities in the region failed to transition their economies effectively into emerging sectors. As a measure of just how quickly the region declined, the Rust Belt accounted for 43% of aggregate employment in 1950 but just 27% in 2000. In terms of manufacturing employment, the Rust Belt share was over one-half in 1950 and just one-third in 2000. In many Rust Belt cities, manufacturing jobs with pay and benefits that allowed a stable middle-class existence were replaced with lower paying part-time jobs in the retail or food service sectors.

Arguably, the storied Carnegie Mellon University was the initial provocateur that activated a local network to stem – then turn around – this period of decline. Both CMU and the University of Pittsburgh used the technologies that were emerging from their respective research initiatives to form the cornerstone of an ecosystem that looked far beyond the steel industry. Using strengths in computing, robotics, and biotechnology, they spurred startup activity that attracted and nurtured a new class of entrepreneurs in the area. Importantly, they cooperated closely with local government institutions as well as industry partners (notably, Uber and Google, both of which now have large offices in Pittsburgh) to pull this off.

By the time 2010 rolled around, Pittsburgh was a city transformed. At the time, it enjoyed an unemployment rate nearly two percentage points lower than the national average, along with 1,600 technology companies and a growing population. Both the storied Robotics Institute and the National

Robotics Engineering Center had gained reputations as leaders in robotics innovation. According to the Brookings Institute, by 2016 the region's per-capita university R&D spending was nearly two and a half times the national average.

Why was Pittsburgh able to pull this off while other cities in a similar situation did not? Several factors are likely at play. First, the city was forced to face the reality of the looming phase change to economic despondency more acutely than many. Seemingly overnight, over 150,000 jobs in manufacturing went away. Second, the city presented itself as livable and lively: Bill Peduto, Pittsburgh's mayor since 2014, attributes the difference to making Pittsburgh into a place where the talent that fuels Pittsburgh's ecosystem actually wants to live. Local charms, coupled with low crime rates and cost of living, and a strong sense of local culture supported by city and state initiatives, formed a reinforcing ecosystem of talent and employers that continues to strengthen. Perhaps most importantly, however, other cities with similar world-class institutions (Johns Hopkins University in Baltimore, for example) failed to form the same broad ecosystems enabled by close collaboration across local government, education, and even cultural and artistic initiatives.

A WORD ON ECOSYSTEMS

Increasingly we are finding that ecosystems are one of the best ways to sense, respond to, and, when appropriate, accelerate a phase change to a more certain – and desirable – future. The willingness to look beyond the four walls of our own organization – to actively work to be less insular and thereby willing to be exposed to external criticism – may be one of the ultimate signs of a provocateur able to overcome humanity's fatal flaws, including the recognition that it's unlikely that any organization has all the possible skills required to shape a better future. Carnegie Mellon tapped into all the players in its cluster – its ecosystem – to activate the future it wanted to see in Pittsburgh, for instance.[2]

Most of us first hear the word "ecosystem" in primary school science class. According to a revered authority on the natural world – National Geographic – an ecosystem is "a geographic area where plants, animals, and other organisms, as well as weather and landscape, work together to form a bubble of life . . . Every factor in an ecosystem depends on every other factor, either directly or indirectly." James Moore is widely credited with bringing the idea of the ecosystem to the business world in his 1993 *Harvard Business Review* article, focused on innovation as the core objective within his initial definition of an ecosystem, but conceptually you can apply the notion of coevolving capabilities toward any business objective. In fact, it is a fundamental strategic choice as any organization considers how to execute its path of provocation. Choice is the critical difference between ecosystems used for business and natural ones. Sea stars don't get to pick which pool they will coexist in with others when the tide recedes. Businesses get to *choose* how and with whom they participate (or not) in ecosystems and what they want to use those relationships for. But unless you have explicitly declared the shape and make-up of the ecosystems you will play in (and those that you will not), then you don't have a strategy. Yet many executives seem to act as if statements like "we will be a part of an ecosystem" are enough.

YOU ARE ALREADY PART OF AN ECOSYSTEM

Try as we might, we can't think of a business that could credibly say it doesn't participate in *any* ecosystem as part of its business model. Any company with a typical supply chain and customers is technically, by virtue of these external partners, part of an ecosystem. But even though they have existed forever in business history, ecosystems suddenly seem to be the hot new thing in management thinking. The idea that creating porous organizational boundaries to access outside talent might create some strategic advantage is not new. Joy's Law – the observation ascribed to Sun Microsystems' Bill Joy that "no matter who you are, most of the smartest people work for someone else" – has been kicking around for over two decades.

What is new is the urgency to access the best possible capabilities as quickly as possible just to survive, let alone to be competitive. Digital giants are working hard to discover ways to leverage their platforms to expand into traditionally well-insulated industries. Smaller upstarts are using technology-driven business models to quickly unseat longstanding incumbents; think how quickly people are substituting in-home connected exercise equipment (e.g., Peloton) for gym memberships, a gradual trend that dramatically accelerated due to COVID-19. Increasingly, if an organization wants to remain competitive, it can't rely on the capabilities it can conceivably create within its four walls. Further, because of technology, it's becoming easier and easier to access the capabilities of outside organizations. So perhaps it's no surprise that the topic of ecosystems is rising quickly on strategy agendas.

Ecosystems are not new, but in the face of this new optionality, it is newly important that leaders need to make clear ecosystem choices. The most foundational choice that organizations need to make as it relates to ecosystems is what to use them for. Although on the surface one could label this a simple choice, it isn't in the least. There are several factors that need to be considered when evaluating whether to do something solely in-house or with one or multiple outside parties as you try to provoke the future you desire. They include:

- How much better (or cheaper) could we deliver against the business objective by working with outside parties?

- How quickly can we build the capability with others versus doing it ourselves?

- If we build the capability with others, can our competition access similar (or even the same) partners to build the same capability?

Ultimately, each choice needs to be examined on its own merit and, sadly, there is no simple formula. There is one rule of thumb that we turn to: if the capability is a critical part of delivering your organization's overall differentiation, then it's more important that that capability be proprietary in nature. If your differentiation lies instead in your ability to convene and lightly orchestrate the activities of many, then virtually nothing other than your word-of-mouth reputation as a force for good need be proprietary. This was the case with Mozilla.

MOZILLA AND THE CROWD AS ECOSYSTEM

Consider the early days of the open-source software movement, when a small collection of individuals upended the business model – and all associated orthodoxies – of making money from tight control of intellectual property (IP) ownership.

The first Internet browser war, which took place during the late 1990s, was a seminal period in modern Internet history. In 1994, computer scientists Marc Andreesen and Jim Clark co-founded Netscape. Building on Andreesen's previous work at the National Center for Supercomputing Applications (NCSA) at the University of Illinois Urbana-Champaign where he had co-created the Internet browser Mosaic, Netscape released Netscape Navigator to the public – the first widely available browser for mass-market Internet users.[3]

Navigator was an instant homerun, earning 75% market share in just four months. Major success followed for the early Internet pioneers at Netscape – growing market share that led to a huge initial public offering (IPO) in 1995. At the time, it seemed Netscape was poised to reap the massive rewards of the impending Internet boom, but that was not to be the case. Software giant Microsoft had been developing their own Internet browser and they had Netscape in their sights. Ironically built on the same architecture as Andreesen's Mosaic, Internet Explorer (IE) challenged Netscape in a war of feature one-upmanship for the next few years. The killer blow to Netscape, however, came when Microsoft started bundling IE with their near-ubiquitous Windows operating system. By 1999, with Microsoft commanding a massive market-share lead, the phase change's shift to "when" meant that Netscape risked becoming irrelevant.

Two years earlier, in 1997, software developer Eric Raymond published "The Cathedral and the Bazaar," a pioneering essay about his experience managing an open-source project and his observations of Linux kernel development. For many within Netscape, this essay was just the nudge they needed to embrace open-source. In 1998, Netscape published the code for the Netscape Communicator 4.0 suite, with the expressed goal to "harness the creative power of thousands of programmers on the Internet by incorporating their best enhancements into future versions of Netscape's software." By making the code public, users around the world could contribute toward feature improvements and updates. After the sale of Netscape to AOL in 1998, AOL gradually phased out browser development as a focus and, instead, the responsibility to take the open-source browser project forward was moved to the nonprofit organization Mozilla Foundation, which spun off from parent Netscape.[4]

The team at Mozilla continued development of the browser, relying on thousands of programmers across the world to aid in the process. A beta was released in 1998, but it wasn't until 2002 that their first browser was ready for the public. The team had first called it Mozilla Phoenix but after legal challenges they eventually settled on Firefox – the first version of which was released on November 9, 2004. It was downloaded over 100 million times within a year. Over the next few years, the popularity of the browser grew steadily, peaking at 32.2% market share by the end of 2009.[5]

Much of the success of Mozilla and Firefox was built on a shrewd calculation by the team to promote conditions that would expressly create advantages for them in the browser market. Specifically, having spun out of Netscape, the team at Mozilla would have known all too well how challenging it would be to compete with huge incumbents that had entrenched advantages in terms of the popularity of their operating system, capital, and large teams of developers. But while Mozilla itself did not have the resources or human capital to compete, they knew they could strike an advantage by relying on thousands of passionate volunteer developers globally to successfully create a product that outperformed existing options. In their own words, by "creating an open community, the Mozilla project had become larger than any one company." Inputs from these contributors – called Mozillians, just like staff – were key in terms of creating a successful product. By introducing pop-up blocking, tabbed browsing, and add-ons, among other features, Firefox 1.0 was significantly more advanced than its main competitor.

A big part of Mozilla's success was their ability to spot the growing open-source trend that they could capitalize on. With examples of open-source movements successfully disrupting established incumbents – such as Linux in the operating system industry and Wikipedia in the encyclopedia and information space – there was a clear trend for Mozilla to take advantage of. Add to this rapidly growing Internet adoption and a growing base of global users with programming and software development skills, and the time was ripe for a successful open-source browser. But while the team at Mozilla had signaled their intent to create an ecosystem of global developers as early as the Netscape Communicator 4.0 launch in 1998, the journey to major launch in 2004 was certainly not easy. It took a high degree of ability from the technical team to create the product itself, but it also involved the added complexity of managing a large, global open-source project that required not just significant participation but also high engagement and quality from volunteers to be successful.

This is no small feat – and perhaps why Mozilla invests so much in terms of building and nurturing its community of developers with offerings such as a dedicated developer version of Firefox and resources that include tools, technical support, forums, and trainings, as well as community building initiatives, campaigns, and events. The continued growth and development of this ecosystem has allowed Mozilla to build a suite of products beyond the Firefox browser in recent years – including Mozilla VPN, Pocket, and Thunderbird, among others.

It is easy to imagine why the team at Mozilla first wanted to name their flagship product after the mythical phoenix. Inspired by its namesake's regenerative power, they imagined their browser rising from the ashes of the first browser war to succeed in this competitive landscape. Built on an ecosystem of volunteers, Mozilla's subsequent success in terms of challenging Internet Explorer's monopoly has allowed the company to soar – while helping create a free and open Internet for all.

Mozilla is but one example of an ecosystem artfully constructed and executed. As the concept of business ecosystems ages, their types and specificity of purpose have blossomed. What used to be blurrily conceived of as some form of working collaboratively with others now has a range of increasingly specific nomenclature and business models. A transaction ecosystem like eBay is fundamentally different from an API ecosystem, which enables the seamless service of Uber, even though both are focused on matching supply with demand.

Platforms have existed in tech for decades and they are now one of the *de rigueur* promises of would-be unicorns seeking funding. Multi-entity partnerships have long supported complex assembly processes such as automotive or aerospace manufacturing. And the more natural definition of self-sufficient interrelationships with built-in redundancy have helped collaborative efforts such as Mozilla or Wikipedia operate at massive scales. The trick for executives these days is to consider the ecosystem options in front of them in a way that allows them to make a choice that leads to advantage from participation in the direction that they have decided to provoke.

We use two dimensions to frame the options and, ultimately, the choice. The first dimension is around the degree to which the ecosystem is proprietary or open. The extreme end of the proprietary spectrum is the bilateral contract, and as you add parties but keep the system closed, you get the multinodal partnership, where there are a small number of players in the ecosystem, each uniquely contributing a specific capability that is unduplicated by the others. At the "open" extreme of the spectrum is what looks more like the "natural" ecosystem from science class. Such a system is likely to have a large number of varied participants, all working together as a system in which the whole is supported, as is each of the individual players. Importantly, room exists for capability overlap among the players and therefore some systemic redundancy. Although participants have varying objectives, no one entity is so critical that the system fails if that entity dies or decides to leave.

The second dimension is the degree to which the ecosystem is intended to be short-term or permanent. Generally, most business structures of the past have relied on the presumption (or illusion) of permanence. With the accelerating rate of change in business models everywhere, however, that is no longer a given. As we struggled to contain and then respond to the dual health and economic emergencies of COVID-19, for instance, we saw largely self-organizing partnerships form for short-term needs. Erstwhile savage competitors in technology and retail worked together toward a common purpose. Traditional supply chain barriers were broken down in favor of achieving systemic efficiency. Most of these were ecosystems of convenience. No one expected these collaborations to exist forever, but for a period of time a number of businesses acted as if it was the new norm.

Bilateral and multinodal partnerships have long been an effective way for a small set of companies to come together with the primary purpose of maximizing profit (even before we called them ecosystems). Typically, profits end up being distributed in rough correlation with the scarcity of the capabilities that are contributed, with the more important or more scarce contribution earning the higher profit. They benefit from being reasonably easy to set up as long as the would-be partners share a clear objective and strict contracts and operating agreements prevent players from infringing on others' turf.

Because these ecosystems are contractual, they require higher coordination and administrative costs, but for many players that may be worth the clear line-of-sight they have to making money in the short term. In the past, long-term deals between participants, each with durable individual competitive advantage, allowed this model to continue undisturbed. But because these are relatively "closed" ecosystems with accelerating change, the advantage they create has a decreasing shelf life – either because competition can increasingly quickly emerge from other consortia that have similar shared objectives (for example, the SkyTeam Alliance vs. the OneTeam alliance vs. the Star Alliance in the airline world) or because the rules and regulations needed to manage the partnership are not nimble enough to absorb changes in the business landscape.

Natural ecosystems, with many participants of each kind, tend to be more resilient than multinodal partnerships. These are self-organizing with no loudest voice, and with some built-in overlap in roles. In these types of ecosystems, the redundancy means that no single participant can count definitively on its fair share but that the long-term viability of the entity is higher: when one part of the system fails, the backups kick in. It's harder for any individual player to make short- to medium-term profit in a natural ecosystem because its unique contribution is lower. But in the face of increasing uncertainty, many companies are willing to hand over some short-term gains in hopes that they thrive for longer. The multiplayer ecosystem that is defined as "Hollywood" (think studios, talent agencies, production lots, writers, directors, actors, etc.) is a prime example.

Activating your ecosystem is one of the few genuinely recursive strategic choices, requiring not just close attention but near-continuous monitoring and revisiting. Every time you make a shift in your strategic choices related to ecosystems, there will be a ripple effect through every other aspect of your strategy. And we are increasingly finding that no company should rest on its business-model laurels in the face of uncertainty. Many learned this the hard way during the COVID-19 pandemic: Who could have imagined that so many entrenched ways of doing business could be so fundamentally undermined in a matter of mere weeks?

We believe that organizations will increasingly value the redundancy and resilience inherent in natural ecosystems that have multiple players of the same type. We may even see a migration from permanent structures to more semi-permanent structures as problems in business evolve at

a faster rate. We hope that our entreaty to provoke – to DO SOMETHING! – will contribute to that migration.

ACCELERATING CHANGE

Speed matters. As the cycle time of change increases, the provocateur who is able to act, assess, and then act again at an accelerating rate is more likely to create advantage. Deciding to act in the face of uncertainty may feel like success in itself. But it is possible to move languorously, with those fatal flaws rearing their heads, and meek moves a shallow cover for not really wanting to provoke a reaction from the outside world. This principle applies to every provocation, and the more you can do to avoid languor, the better.

Follow-through, courage of conviction, commitment: all of these are required for a provocation to "count." And for those who are truly interested in driving change in the world, there are a variety of approaches to accelerating cycle time of both individual moves and those of the whole system. Repeatedly acting through or with accelerators can bring about our desired future sooner and in starker relief than what otherwise might have been the case.

Many of the accelerators that can help are going to be familiar with today's popular management thinking. To name a few:

- *Agile operations and prototyping*: In its broadest connotation, this is simply aligning everyone to the importance of acting quickly in a test-and-learn mindset, working with low-fidelity approximations of solutions to enable faster and more accurate market feedback. Arguably, those who are able to actually pull this off (as opposed to simply talking about its importance) can use it as a fleeting source of advantage.

- *Big Data and AI*: Though we're not fans of using it as the only source of insight about the outside world, the variety of tools in this catch-all bucket can help spot patterns early in data coming back from market tests, speeding up and deepening learning in the process.

- *Influencers and market mavens*: The slightly more human and analog version of AI, maintaining a network of advisors who sit on the cutting edge of the way certain markets are unfolding, can help you keep provocations on track by acting as early-warning systems if you appear to be off-track from the intended market reaction.

These are just a few and, undoubtedly, more will arrive on the scene as exponential change enables ever-more-impressive technological support of human efforts. But we're pretty sure that the value of ecosystems will endure through all that change. Not only do they provide us an extended and interconnected sensing network to hear market signals better and faster, but by definition they expand optionality as we consider different execution moves on any path of provocation.

In terms of structured guidance – to the extent we feel we can offer some – on how to provoke with purpose, that's about all we have. But just as all the ideas in this book were born from our experiences watching our clients struggle to advance in the face of uncertainty, some successfully and some less successfully, we think stories of others are the most powerful mechanisms to make the point. For Part III of our book, we decided to turn to the experts: those who have guided their own organizations down a path of provocation that achieved their objectives. All of them have done so in a way and with an outcome that has had a profoundly positive impact in the broader world around them.

PART III

PROFILES OF PROVOCATEURS

Many of the stories we have shared thus far have to do with business executives taking action in the corporate world – whether in established companies or in start-ups. But leadership is not confined to companies, and we're firm believers in the value of lateral learning – that is, taking lessons from one context and applying them to a completely different one as a source of novel insight and advantage.

The provocateurs we have chosen for this part of the book are thus purposely not famous (or infamous) business titans. Indeed, the casual onlooker may not immediately recognize the degree to which they are in fact extraordinary – people who have provoked important change that has made the world a better place in ways they themselves never would have imagined.

One comes from the world of nonprofits, one from the civic sector, and one from the public and private finance sector. But a connective thread binds them: all three stories revolve around the world's continuing mandate to build organizations and societies that are more diverse, equitable, and inclusive, and that enable more positive human connections between individuals. Beyond their surface-level value of just being the right things to strive for, these objectives, as we discussed earlier in the book, also lead to better decision-making and resilience in organizations that face uncertainty of all types.

Everyone – no matter your organization, position, age, or background – can take a lesson or two away from the stories of Debbie, Ryan, and Valerie.

CHAPTER 10

Deborah Bial

Chauncy Street in Cambridge, Massachusetts, is pretty much exactly what you would expect from a street nestled in the heart of Harvard University. Four- and five-story prewar brick buildings intermingle with trees along the short, wide, one-way street connecting Garden Street to Massachusetts Avenue. It's rare enough that anyone has the good fortune to be accepted at Harvard, and rarer still to live on Chauncy Street while there. With Radcliffe a stone's throw in one direction and Harvard Law School a stone's throw in the other, students are within walking distance of almost anywhere they might need to be on campus.

We wonder what the chances are, then, that someone matriculates at Harvard twice and ends up living on Chauncy both times, at the same address, in the same apartment. It turns out that with the right conditions in place, it's not nearly as unlikely as we would have thought.

Deborah Bial is best known as the founder and president of The Posse Foundation. As she has built Posse into what it is today, over 30 years after its inception, her path has been punctuated by accomplishments and experiences that many can only dream of. She is a recipient of the MacArthur Foundation "genius" grant. She invented a college adaptability index and has received over 25 honorary doctorates. President Obama donated part of his Nobel Peace Prize money to assist Debbie's cause; a decade later, so did MacKenzie Scott, who gave Posse a grant of $10 million. Debbie has helped over 10,000 students from diverse backgrounds to attend and graduate from college, coordinating over $1.5 billion in tuition funding along the way. She is a trustee of Brandeis University.

Oh, and she attended Harvard twice: once for a master's degree, once for a doctorate. The story of how Debbie ended up living in the same apartment with the huge windows on the first floor of 18 Chauncy Street both times provides a neat little glimpse into how she thinks and operates and helps explain the provocateur behind this amazing string of accomplishments.

Before reading the story, though, it's important that you understand the type of person Debbie is. When you first meet her, you know beyond the shadow of a doubt that she is intensely interested in you and in getting to know you better. She is open, warm, quick to smile, and deeply skilled at quickly finding common ground to make anyone in a conversation feel more comfortable opening up and engaging. She connects to people and likes to connect them to each other. She looks you directly in the eye when you're speaking, her face slightly creased with the beginnings of a smile, and when she asks you something we swear she actually has some way to make her eyes twinkle just a little bit more. She probes constantly, always seeking to understand why you think and believe what you do, to know what in your background might have influenced your worldview to shape you into the person in front of her. If there's a pause in dinner conversation, she'll hit the table with a zinger of a question that will in all likelihood plunge everyone into a deep state of introspection – and then debate – before parting ways sometime later with a bunch of new best friends. And she hugs. A lot.

We can only imagine what happened behind the scenes as Debbie was searching for housing during her second stint at Harvard. Since leaving Cambridge with her Masters, she had often thought back to her ground floor apartment at 18 Chauncy Street. She loved the location. She loved being able to look out at the trees in summer and the snow in winter. More than anything, she loved the light that shone in through the big windows facing the street. Naturally, the first place she asked her real estate agent to show her was her old address. Sadly, she quickly found out that while there was indeed a vacant unit at the address, her old apartment was being lived in by a young man and his fiancée, settled in comfortably on the cusp of their new life together. Debbie agreed to see the third-floor apartment, but even though it was bigger, it just wasn't the same: not the same feel, not the same view, and definitely not the same light. She didn't want it.

Several weeks later, Debbie was living in her old apartment and the engaged guy had moved – fiancée and all – to the vacant third-floor apartment. When we first heard this story, we were both stumped about what might have transpired. Debbie's not overtly aggressive, she doesn't have money to throw around to get her way, she generally likes to avoid conflict, and she's usually looking for any and every way to make others happy.

What we have found out is this: Debbie walked out of the building with the disappointed realtor who just didn't understand the rejection in such a tight rental market. She waited until he walked away, then she did a 180 and walked back into the building and knocked on the door of her old apartment. When the occupants answered the door, she introduced herself.

"Hi, I'm Debbie. I used to live here . . . and I would really love to live here again."

She paused to watch their reaction, and then, she told us:

"I just asked."

Over the course of a series of interviews (during which, we might note, it felt as though we were interviewees as often as interviewers), we have gotten to know Debbie and the story of her success both personally and with The Posse Foundation in much more detail. She has been careful to note that those two stories are not the same, and that there are lots of other people who have helped build Posse alongside her. But there's no doubt that without Debbie, there would be no Posse in the form that exists today. From the first time she had an inkling about what Posse could become close to three and a half decades ago, she has been the primary mover to provoke the future that she desired for herself and those around her. Her default mode is to drive, but it's clear that whether she knew she was doing it or not, she has used all the modes of provocation to her benefit at different points over time.

Posse is, as Debbie puts it, a "diversity and leadership development program whose long-term goal is to build a leadership network for the United States that is more reflective of the demographics of the population." It is based on its two foundational theories – one of leadership and the other of change. As Debbie told a class at HBS, "Individuals who think about how aspects of identity (including race, gender, class, sexuality, and religion) relate to decision-making become stronger leaders – in the workplace and in the world at large. By increasing the numbers of Posse alumni in leadership positions in the workforce, the quality of leadership will improve. Their decision-making will reflect the voices, the needs, the interests of all Americans."[1]

The idea – and the name – came from an experience Debbie had when she was working, soon after graduating from Brandeis University, in an after-school program called the CityKids Foundation. Founded in 1985, CityKids is a youth repertory program primarily involving highly talented, diverse young people from the New York City public school system. In her role with the nonprofit, Debbie was often struck by the talent of the teenagers that she was working with, capable of anything they set their minds to despite some of them having had limited access to resources while growing up. Many went on to college, some winning scholarships, only to return to the city because college felt like a complete culture shock. One such student remarked on returning home, "You know, I never would have dropped out of college if I had my posse with me."

At the time, Debbie notes, "the word *posse* was in the vernacular . . . a popular word to represent 'my cohort,' 'my group of friends,' 'the people who back me up.' It just made so much sense! Why not send a team of students together to college so that they can back each other up? So that way if you grew up in the Bronx and you ended up in Middlebury, Vermont, you would be less likely to say, 'I don't want to stay here' and leave."

From that early inkling of an idea, Posse has blossomed. And while the term may have faded in popularity, Debbie's vision has only brightened and tightened. At its heart, Posse is and has always been a merit-based program whose mission is to identify, recruit, and train high schoolers in the United States with extraordinary leadership potential. These Posse Scholars then receive full-tuition leadership scholarships from Posse's partner colleges and universities when they attend school in groups of 10 – the eponymous posse. Before heading off to school, Scholars take part in Posse's precollegiate training (PCT) program to prepare them. Once on campus, Posse uses a variety of formal and informal approaches to support Scholars preparing for and transitioning into the workforce, connecting them with career coaches, internships, and jobs.

Two of the foundational elements of the program are the "Dynamic Assessment Process" (DAP) and the PossePlus Retreat (PPR). DAP is Posse's unique approach to identifying and selecting scholars. It uses a mix of intergroup activities that allow Posse to look for signals of promise well beyond traditional metrics like the SAT and school grades. DAP taps into local connections with urban public schools and community organizations to reach a diverse pool of talented students with high leadership potential. What's special about the interview process itself is that the group-based, task-oriented applicant experiences highlight noncognitive interactive and communication skills; the interviews focus on behavioral stories from the past instead of just on-the-spot tests of aptitude and self-reported beliefs and accomplishments. The matching process between Scholars and schools accounts for preferences on both sides to ensure a good fit.

The PPR is an off-campus experience facilitated by Posse for each of the partner schools. Across the country more than 5,000 college students participate in PPRs annually. At the retreats, every Scholar is asked to invite one non-Posse student to join them along with faculty and administrators to discuss an important social-political issue – one identified through a national survey of Scholar interests every year. These two core elements of the programming work toward driving the change necessary to achieve the ultimate organizational goal.

These core aspects of the program have remained rock-solid as the organization has matured and expanded in its mission and impact. Notably, the first STEM Posse was created in 2007, followed five years later by a post-9/11 veterans' Posse program. Now that the majority of Posse Scholars are out in the workforce, you will find Debbie and the Posse staff talking more frequently of the focus on leadership in the workforce, rather than just leadership on campus. Posse Consulting was launched in 2014 as a mechanism to accelerate positive culture change in business, government, and nonprofit organizations on a fee-for-service basis by offering training, best practices, and learning from Posse's experience over the past three decades. And at the time of this writing, there are other exciting changes in a design and prototype stage.

By 2020, when the tumult of the year opened up new opportunities for the organization, Posse had grown to involve more than 60 top-tier partner colleges and universities including Cornell, Pepperdine, and Northwestern. On top of the numbers of students involved and scholarships provided, referenced previously, other impressive figures include:

- 17,000 nominations and $150 million in scholarships awarded annually
- Chapters in 10 major cities around the United States
- 200+ board and advisory board members
- $100 million+ in assets

And perhaps the most impressive statistic of all: over 90% of Posse Scholars persist and graduate from college, almost 50% better than the overall national average of 62%.

Put simply: Posse works.

Debbie can rattle off the names of dozens of people who played even bit parts in the Posse journey. But she has been the driver of Posse's mission, the creator of its core principles and programming, and at the heart of every major step, driving outcomes in ways that we're sure those around her never knew she was. If you delve into Debbie's deeper history, you will hear the stories and see the patterns that are imprinted indelibly on Posse today.

Debbie was born in Manhattan and grew up in Teaneck, New Jersey, the daughter of a contra-bassoonist for the New York Philharmonic orchestra and an information officer for the New York State Psychiatric Institute. She remembers a pretty middle-class experience in a "white house with red shutters," walking to school, doing fine but not at the top of her class. She was a rule-follower who wanted to please her parents and her teachers. She was a "skinny kid . . . who couldn't wait for dinner to be over so [she] could go read [her] book."

But there's much more below that surface-level story, slight dichotomies that provide signals about her particular mode of doing something. She was a rule follower who went out of her way to say hello to strangers on her walks to school. She was a teacher-pleaser who once picked a fight with an elementary school librarian who tried to prevent her from checking out a book intended for the grade above hers. She was an introvert who wrote a play in third grade to be performed for everyone in her school. Above all, perhaps, she was an empath through and through, often going so far as to ascribe feelings to inanimate objects: "Even if I didn't like some clothes," she told us, "I would wear them because I didn't want them to feel bad."

When Debbie graduated from Brandeis University, she returned to New York to work as a trainer with CityKids. Before the fateful remark about posses and dropping out of college, though, through her work Debbie was exposed to a powerful reality that set the context for her wanting to take action. The kids she was working with were smart, supertalented, wanted to go to college, and as deserving of a top-notch university education as anyone. But they weren't presented with a pathway to a better future. "They weren't getting connected," Debbie says, "because the way we were defining who 'deserved' to attend the top colleges was too narrow . . . and that was a missed opportunity." She also came to understand the power of exposing this talent to decision makers firsthand.

As Debbie describes it:

It was really fun to work there at the time. They were connected to all of these celebrities like Demi Moore, Bruce Willis, and Richard Gere. Keith Haring had done their logo. The kids were coming from the public schools to this after school program where they were writing and producing theatre and music. I was just out of college running leadership workshops with the kids . . . and there was something that we were producing called "speak-outs." We would get 400 students together in a room like a ballroom in a hotel. They'd spend a whole day speaking out on an issue that they cared about: they spoke about their school experiences, their communities, their lives. . . . They wrote performance pieces

about global warming, the environment, the justice
system. They performed these pieces and . . . they
were so good that these celebrities got involved.

She realized that watching supertalented young people
accomplish new things motivated *everyone*: people working in
the social sector and also people in business, entertainment,
and government; rich people and poor people; never-to-be-
famous people and famous people. The programming led to an
expanding web of connections with influential people, and
eventually to the visit of some deans and professors from
Peabody College at Vanderbilt University. Debbie told us, "We
invited some of the Vanderbilt people to Leonard Street, to the
basement offices, and they saw what we were working on. They
were blown away by the kids – we all saw their talent, we saw
their brilliance, we saw their brains . . . and they left and said,
'We want those kids on our campus.'" Something in the assessment methods that schools like Vanderbilt were using in their
admission protocols was leading them to miss these high-
impact applicants.

There was the signal, and Debbie caught it, leading to the
establishment of a pilot program at Vanderbilt – the seed that
would lead to the establishment of The Posse Foundation. In
the early years, there were bouts of doubt, no pay, and naysay-
ers, but the signal mattered. It was the appearance of an "if"-to-
"when" trend and served as Debbie's seminal envision
provocation. She saw the possibility that an idea like Posse
could work as college campuses continued to struggle with a
lack of diversity in all its dimensions. There may be a way to
help them while helping "the kids" get the types of experiences
they deserved. It was far from certain, but it was possible. And
Debbie set herself to connecting people to give it the greatest
possible chance it could have. The position phase for Debbie
was all about landing the first successful experience.

In 1990, the first "posse" (although there were only 5 students instead of the now-customary 10) took a Greyhound bus from New York City to Nashville, Tennessee. The kids had never set foot on the campus before. There were Confederate flags hanging in the dorm room windows. You could buy a bobblehead doll of a Black person with a watermelon on her head in the gas station down the street. In that white, Southern environment, their arrival was such a big deal that the front page of *The Nashville Scene* had a headline that read, "A Story of 5 Hispanics and Their Experiment at Vanderbilt." Debbie said, "Was it easy, did it just work right away? Of course not! But when human beings believe in something and when you have relationships, and when you believe the idea is good, you fight to make it work. We were not going to fail."

And that, essentially, is the story of Debbie as a provocateur. It's nowhere near the complete story, but it is the essence of what she has done to drive action in the more than 30 years since. She has always been ready to act, to DO SOMETHING! when she has the opportunity. And while she would never call it a playbook, there is a pattern: she is constantly prepared to act, waiting for conditions to shift in whatever way will allow her to advance her mission, biding her time by connecting people and expanding her network in whatever way she can. When conditions do shift, she immediately follows through and takes the next step to drive to the outcome she desires.

When we asked her what her secret is to hitting the targets she aims for, she said, "It's simple: put something on the calendar and hold people accountable for getting there."

Those conditions have shifted a lot over the years. Whether precipitated by a target partner university's changing administrators or the president of the United States donating part of his Nobel Peace Prize money, Debbie is always ready to act. Eight years into the Posse journey, she had the opportunity to speak with *New York Times* opinion columnist Bob Herbert. In true Debbie form, she refused to do a simple telephone interview and convinced Bob to come downtown to meet the kids, which he did. As Debbie tells it, the resultant column legitimized Posse as an organization and put it on the national stage in a way that it had never been before. Two years later, Posse was given a grant from the U.S. Department of Education to open a site in Boston, the first replication site. After that, Posse opened in a new city almost every other year in a steady expansion around the country, which would carry on for the ensuing 15 years. Oh, and Bob and Debbie ended up getting married . . . which, we're sure, is a story for another time.

Clearly, things have not always gone as Debbie would have liked. Posse has faced some heart-wrenching challenges along the way. On September 11, 2001, Posse's offices were four blocks from the terrorist disaster that unfolded at the World Trade Center. They were scheduled to hold a national training for all their staff in advance of an upcoming DAP and literally had people in the air from Boston and Chicago in airplanes, looking down on the devastating scene below. Debbie made desperate attempts to get downtown after the first plane hit, giving up on the shut-down subway to cajole a cab driver to take her farther and farther south - until the second plane hit and "the blood just rushed out of [her] body."

Through a teary breakdown, Debbie gathered herself in order to stay strong . . . and started to act. She organized for staff to haul all their training materials to her apartment. The next day, they were on her rooftop developing a plan of action to still carry through with DAP; they couldn't cancel it and let the kids down. Debbie called Gaston Caperton, the former governor of West Virginia, who was the president of the College Board at the time. She secured an invitation to temporarily relocate to the College Board's offices, where Posse stayed for the next six weeks. And they didn't miss a beat. Debbie recounts,

> That year, I remember feeling panic and grief. I remember the horrible scene of people jumping out of the windows of World Trade Center. I remember Giuliani allowing people who worked on Wall Street to go back downtown; we had to walk from City Hall wearing masks. It was like a nuclear holocaust down there . . . we walked into our offices and everything – even the pens, every phone – was covered in this fine dust from the toppled World Trade Center and it was devastating. But we did not say "we're going to skip this year" or "we're going to just close for a while"; we kept on working. We did not miss work. We didn't miss a day.

Fast-forward almost 20 years. Speaking with Debbie as the events of 2020 played out is a fascinating study in what *actually* happens in the real life of even the best provocateurs. For everyone, times of upheaval are messy and confusing and anxiety producing, and 2020 entailed a string of upheavals that seemed to never end. The two whose fallout seems set to change the destiny of Posse the most, though, are the sudden virtualization of the United States because of the COVID-19 outbreak in March and the murder of George Floyd just two months later.

By the time early 2020 had rolled around, Posse was, by definition, a high-touch organization. Scholars were recruited only from the cities where there were local offices because DAP and the precollege, after-school program required people getting together in a room. And the system worked, as evidenced by the accelerating successes of Posse Scholars through all walks of life. Although Debbie and the rest of the Posse staff had been tempted to think of other growth strategies over time, the cost/benefit balance of further physical expansion didn't make sense, and there had been no signal that the world was capable of shifting inherently in-person experiences to the virtual world. And then, suddenly, the signal was there. We all learned how to Zoom, and Posse itself was forced to conduct its activities over video – and it continued to work.

Debbie saw a new idea that could dramatically increase Posse's impact. Their virtual model meant that Posse could recruit students from any city. Not only that, but she could now establish geographically diverse cohorts – a potential game changer for the organization's expansion goals. Debbie did what she does and picked up the phone, calling Arne Duncan, the Secretary of Education for the United States during the Obama administration, and Alberto Carvalho, the superintendent of the Miami Dade public school system. She asked them to rally support from the superintendents of the school systems in major cities where Posse was not present, to have them join her on a call to launch a new idea of a virtual Posse.

"All the superintendents we invited came," Debbie reports, "and they all said 'of course we'll help: we'd love Posse to come find our kids, we have great kids in our schools' . . . and all those superintendents agreed to send a communication out to every single high school principal in their district and ask them to nominate students. At the same time, [she] started calling college presidents and guess what . . . they liked the idea of geographically diverse Posses; they wanted to do it."

But, of course, COVID-19 was not the only precipitating factor in play at the time. Posse has always operated at the intersection of higher education and diversity and has been able to shift as times have changed. It evolved as the various aspects and benefits of the concept of "diversity" gained a more concrete and sophisticated language system. Debbie is the first to admit that she, too, has changed over her 30-odd year history with Posse. She notes, "I am much more inspired and committed now by a core sense of social justice than I was when I was 23 years old and Posse started. What was moving me at the time was the human connection with these kids. Right now, what moves me is a feeling of deep injustice."

With the murder of George Floyd in May 2020, the reality of systemic racism finally snapped to the forefront of public consciousness. With it, Debbie's vehement adherence to a core concept of Posse – its basis on merit – became crystal clear in its importance to anyone who previously might have seen it as just one fuzzy component of the whole model. Debbie says,

White people in this country have had a history of looking at people of color, especially Black people, like they are all in need of help or charity, like they are all in need of remediation, like they are in need of fixing. We have a history of using deficit-based programs for "kids at risk" or for underprivileged, underserved students – often students of color – to achieve diversity goals in our colleges and universities. And while these programs are important, when they are the primary way we aim to achieve diversity, we create a kind of caste among college students: those who are there based on their merits and those who have been permitted to attend out of charity. Posse is a diversity initiative with merit at its core – with the idea that a merit scholarship should be about more than a test score; that leadership and multiracial skill sets are critical to a healthy

campus community and that those who bring those
skill sets are valued as much as a top violinist, a star
quarterback or [a] student with top SAT scores.
Integrated diversity is a value that includes all students and all students deserve equally to be part.
This is really important. I challenge you to find one
other program in the United States, one other
diversity initiative that is a national, merit-based
program. We are that one. We are that program.

Despite all the uncertainties that 2020 threw at Debbie
and Posse – how could a remote model even work? what
would happen to funding as the economy disintegrated?
would people miss the point about Posse's central role in pre-
venting injustice? – they emerged stronger and with a range
of different options on paths forward. Helped in myriad
ways by a large, public grant from the MacKenzie Scott
Foundation in the middle of the year, Debbie was ready to
DO SOMETHING! again, this time more directly intervening with large organizations.

Debbie says,

Posse has always been a leadership program, but it
was heavily focused on the support. We believed
that you could support students through the edu-
cational process so they can go be leaders. Now as
we are about to pick our 10,000th Posse Scholar,
we are shifting our energy into the leadership piece
more directly . . . Our country is so polarized and
the leaders that we are looking at out there are
from a narrow slice of the population; 90% of the
United States Senate is white and 75% of senators
are men. When are we going to see change? Are we

just going to say, well, we need to fix our K–12 system? We can't wait for that. I am now looking at companies that care a lot about diversity, equity, and inclusion. They build programs to support that value but almost all of those programs focus on entry-level internships and opportunities. I'm wondering why we don't see the investment at the top. Why aren't the executive leadership teams building internship programs at that level? Why don't we see CEOs and CFOs and the rest of the C-suite, and the people right below them, engaged in this as well?

Debbie clearly understands Posse's special place in the work that needed to be done in *all* organizations, not just universities. Posse, at its core, had always been about a multiracial approach to fighting racism and to building integrated communities. Its 30-year track record positioned the organization as a leader in action and change. Suddenly, Posse was receiving phone calls and requests from colleges and universities interested in joining the program and companies wanting to hire Posse to deliver diversity, equity, and inclusion training. Posse's approach had a definition of merit that included leadership and that became critically important in the national conversation about equity and antiracism.

Debbie will continue to drive outcomes that fit her vision for the future. And while that vision may evolve over time, our guess is that some aspects of how she moves will not. She will not compromise on the fundamentals of Posse simply to make short-term gains. She will continue to be first to see the "if"-to-"when" and immediately pick up the phone to start to connect people to position for success. And then she'll start putting things on the calendar.

Chances are you'll be hearing a lot more about the Posse Foundation in the years to come and may even be one of the people Debbie calls in her ever-expanding web of connections. We just hope that if you're living on the first floor of 18 Chauncy Street in Cambridge when she comes calling, she's not looking for a place to live.

CHAPTER 11

Ryan Gravel

Given our line of business, we've both traveled a lot over the years to places both exotic and decidedly less so. And, like many, we share a habit when visiting a new city of always making it a point to get out and walk: Steve because he's naturally curious, and Geoff because his Dad convinced him years ago that doing so is a surefire cure for jetlag. We're not the only ones who swear by it; there's something about walking a city that moving at faster speeds just doesn't allow for. You get more detail – more of the grit, the smells (good and bad), and definitely more of the beauty.

We have each been blessed to have seminal experiences and memories based on city travels. For Geoff, Tokyo stands out. When he used to travel there regularly, he would typically get out of his sleepless bed before daylight and, just as dawn was breaking, walk down to the Tsukiji Fish Market. Although it has now been shut down and moved to Toyosu, Tsukiji was for decades one of the world's great wonders: a sprawling warren of stalls chock full of unimaginable sea creatures in crates and barrels that seemed to stretch forever. He would quite literally get lost wandering for hours, taking in the mayhem and occasional tuna auction as a cultural and circadian reset.

Steve vividly remembers a 2005 guided tour of Rocinha, a Rio de Janeiro favela that was, at the time, considered one of the most dangerous places in the world. Although much of what he saw was shocking given his background, the tour guide – a local – invited Steve into his home at the end and gave him hope for the future. While outside lay incredible strife and squalor, inside the guide's children were learning on the Internet, something that wouldn't have been possible even a few years earlier.

Ryan Gravel's city epiphany came during study abroad in Paris. That epiphany is now changing the face of his hometown of Atlanta. Known to some as "The BeltLine Guy," Ryan has been on a mission for over two decades to bring a new way of living in and experiencing the city – not to mention the value of human connection – to all Atlantans. What started as a master's thesis at Georgia Tech has turned into one of the largest urban economic development projects in America today, all inspired by a series of wanderings that Ryan experienced in Paris. Along the way, he has had successes both large and small, become pretty famous in Atlanta and beyond, and written a book called *Where We Want to Live: Reclaiming Infrastructure for a New Generation of Cities*. But he has also faced innumerable twists, turns, and failures. Working at the intersection of civic leadership, local and state government, real estate development, the broader private sector, and community activism, Ryan has become the epitome of an Adapt provocateur: always with the end goal in mind and always ready to shift his next step forward to accomplish it.[1]

Many outside the United States – or even outside the state of Georgia for that matter – may not know much about the project that Ryan provoked. Today, the Atlanta BeltLine is envisioned as "the catalyst for making Atlanta a global beacon for equitable, inclusive, and sustainable city life." The goals that the organization lays out are both impressive and daunting: 33 miles of multi-use urban trails; 22 miles of pedestrian-friendly rail transit; $10 billion in economic development; 5,600 units of affordable workforce housing; 1,300 acres of new greenspace; 1,100 acres of environmental cleanup; 46 miles of improved streetscapes; the largest outdoor public art exhibition in the southern United States; and 30,000 permanent jobs. And it all originated in the brain of a college kid who was so caught up in wandering the streets of Paris that he missed his train.[2]

Gravel was born at an Air Force base in Louisiana, where all of his extended family is from. He moved with his immediate family to the suburbs of Atlanta as a toddler because his parents were looking for greater economic opportunity. A twin, Ryan calls himself the "shy and creative one," juxtaposed to a brother whom he describes as athletic, outgoing, and whom all the girls liked. He reports having spent much of his youth "in [his] head imagining things . . . always drawing and making stuff." A self-proclaimed railway nut, he grew up in Chamblee, Georgia, listening to the nearby rail cars go by at night. With a construction engineer as a father and a mother who worked on quilts and crafts, Ryan seems genetically predisposed to fields that blended art and science.

Gravel has also always been fascinated by people. He thinks there is something inherently interesting in the choices people make about their lives and the manifest differences that appear when you look across a community. It's perhaps not surprising, then, that he gravitated toward architecture as his field of study: it managed to check the "art + science" box while giving Ryan the opportunity to design spaces for people to enjoy, move around in, and live their lives in. He describes architecture as three-dimensional problem solving and architectural education as the defense of your design to a jury of peers.

In his senior year at Georgia Tech, Ryan did a year abroad in Paris and "it fundamentally changed the way [he] saw the world." He was there to study architecture, but Ryan quickly learned that "the buildings are indistinguishable from the experience of the city." He recognized that in some ways, architecture was the design of the city. Ryan took to walking everywhere, gazing up and around, perhaps subconsciously working to satiate his natural desire to observe others and his surroundings. Ryan also quickly discovered three things that have long drawn visitors from other parts of the world to Europe: it's relatively small, it's jammed with history and incredibly interesting cities other than Paris, and it's all interconnected with an excellent railway infrastructure.

Ryan had become a student of cities.

As he took all of this in, he observed another phenomenon: he felt better. Within the first month of living there, he lost 15 pounds. He was walking everywhere, eating fresh food, and utterly thriving in the stimulating environment of a bustling city. He was surrounded by incredible architecture and art and – most importantly – a whole society. As he describes it:

> The role of the city in shaping my health and well-being was clear to me in a way that it hadn't been before . . . While I was walking, I was watching. Watching how people lived their lives . . . The city provided a way for people to live the kinds of lives they wanted. Paris opened a door to a different way of living – the kind of life that *I* wanted. It was just so different from the way that I had grown up.

Ryan came to understand that "infrastructure was the construction not only of the city, but of our lives." It's all about the infrastructure. He remembers that within a block of his apartment in Paris, he could walk down the street and make a choice about whether to hop on the metro to go across town or catch a train to Lyon or Berlin. He didn't have to get into a car to go anywhere and, partly as a result, he didn't have to overly plan his life. He could just live it. One of his most formative experiences in Paris also says a lot about Ryan himself and what may lie at the heart of his particular style of provocation.

It happened as he set off on a long weekend. Although he had spent lots of time wandering and observing Paris, his schoolwork had limited his travel in Europe. As his time wound down before having to head back to the States, he planned a lightning-quick jaunt to Pisa and Florence: two Italian cities he had wanted to see for their contributions to culture and architecture. To say that Ryan strikes us as someone who doesn't worry too much about planning things is an understatement, for sure. But this one he had planned: his departure from the Gare de Lyon with two nights at hostels and an overnight train back to Paris would get him back to school in time. Sadly – or perhaps fortuitously – an oversight related to the European norm of conveying times using a 24-hour clock rather than the 12-hour clock that he had grown up with meant that he missed the train for the first leg of his trip by two hours. Late at night, he realized that there was no way that he would be able to fit all he had planned in if he left the next day. But after a few moments of despondency, he ran to another train station across the Seine, to catch a train to Toulouse.

Toulouse is nowhere near Italy, but at least it was south of Paris, which tells us something about Ryan the provocateur. Although he had an objective in mind, he did not define that objective in the way that many might. He didn't define success as reaching Pisa and Florence; he defined it as having an experience that put him in a different place, in the flow with others. While he did eventually make it to Italy that weekend, he had other experiences wandering Toulouse, Nice, and Marseilles. And he's pretty sanguine about the whole thing: "Was I bummed that I had less than a day to see the great masterworks? Sure. But I also experienced things I would never have seen if my trip had gone according to plan."

When we pointed out to him the irony of someone who has built his reputation as an urban planner discounting the value of planning, his response gives us some insight into the brain of Ryan Gravel: "I trust myself to make decisions. You know, like, intuitively, I know kind of where I'm going and I'm super-honest with myself and I just trust myself to make decisions, and that has worked for me so far." He pays attention to signals and he lets those signals define a North Star to strive for, recognizing that he doesn't need to know the exact progression of every step that will take him there. The signals he received in Paris and other parts of Europe planted the seeds that would become the Atlanta BeltLine.

When Gravel returned to Atlanta in 1999, it didn't take too long for his epiphany. He was driving to work on the highway one day when it hit him: he wasn't interacting with anyone the way he did in Paris. He got into his car to go to work and "even though [he] was passing 100,000 people, [he] didn't see anyone. It was mind-numbing. It took about the same amount of time to get to work as it took . . . to get to school in Paris, but [he] didn't move a muscle. [He] realized that the infrastructure [in Atlanta] was a barrier to the kind of life [he] wanted." He saw a fundamental difference between the life he experienced growing up and the life he had enjoyed in Paris. In his words:

> I told you that when I was a kid, I was in my head a lot . . . I lived in my imagination. I think that what happened when I went to Paris was that I saw the real world is actually pretty awesome. Where I grew up, I was observing the squirrels in the trees out our back window . . . which is totally beautiful and cool, but I didn't see people – I didn't understand what they do. And people are actually really interesting . . . and the art and the culture that they create; the diversity

and all the craziness that happens in a real city is really fascinating and really beautiful to me. I learned that in Paris. What you're looking at, basically, is civilization. It's a society. You can put different words to it in terms of "planner speak," but you're basically looking at . . . people living their lives in really interesting ways. Cities have a way of cultivating those lives and giving people opportunities to live the kinds of lives they want.

Ryan didn't know it at that moment, but he was setting the wheels in motion to transform the city of Atlanta.

Ryan worked in architecture for a year after receiving his undergraduate degree but came to realize that the structures he was designing – office complexes built for driving commuters – were part of the problem. So he decided to return to Georgia Tech for a master's in city planning, which later expanded to include a dual degree with architecture. Still dissatisfied with his way of life at the time, and in need of creating a thesis project that would span both planning and design, Ryan decided to do something about it. "I just decided to design the kind of place I'd like to live," Ryan recounts. "I didn't think we were actually going to do it."

One could argue that there are few cities in the world where geography, history, and social issues collide in a way to create the unique context that Atlanta did for Ryan's master's thesis. Ryan's natural interest in railroads (from lying in bed growing up in Chamblee, listening to the passing trains) came into play as it was the technology on which the city of Atlanta had relied for movement of both goods and people in the pre-automobile era.

But to really understand Atlanta, you have to place yourself in the time the city experienced much of its growth: at the same time the automobile was becoming standard in American life, starting in the 1960s and lasting through the next several decades. Most of Atlanta was really designed for cars, not people. "The infrastructure in Atlanta did not include sidewalks for years and years and years. You could develop a whole community, a thousand homes, and not build a single sidewalk," says Ed McBrayer of the PATH Foundation.[3] Atlanta was a collection of disconnected neighborhoods, not laid out in a grid pattern. As a consequence, as a city resident you rarely had an opportunity to interact with your neighbors. And at the time of Ryan's studies, much of downtown Atlanta – where Georgia Tech is located – was still scarred by the loss of industrial activity that had not yet been replaced.

Ryan envisioned a better Atlanta, one where people could walk and ride bikes to go to work, or to the park, or grocery shopping. It was a place to see other people, and a place where people could meet their neighbors. This last concept has always been important to Ryan. He saw that the physical infrastructure in Atlanta, including railroads, divided neighborhoods along lines of race and class and he knew that rethinking those barriers could create an organic way to reconnect with one another.

The basic concept of the BeltLine is to connect 45 different neighborhoods in a loop around the city, leveraging four different railway freight corridors, known as "belt lines," that were built over a century ago and that roughly line up to create a 22-mile loop. Once realized, it would connect these neighborhoods with a combination of trails, transit, parks, art, affordable housing, an arboretum, and a slew of shops and restaurants to enjoy along the way. The concept has been to build this over space that had largely been forgotten in the sprawl that Atlanta had become, to make use of deserted industrial land that deepened divisions between different parts of Atlanta and the citizens themselves. Perhaps most importantly to

Ryan's vision, the BeltLine means that people from areas of Atlanta who would never previously have run into each other are now thrust into the same space to interact.

Ryan's vision wasn't entirely new. There were early plans in the 1960s for some interior commuter lines on portions of the loop, including a train running by the former Sears fortress-looking building. But Ryan's vision included the entire loop and aligned with the kind of future that he – and a lot of other people – were looking for. His thesis described a city with "side-by-side streetcar tracks, 45 stops, dense residential construction, green space and walking trails," based on the idea that "the expansion of mass transit infrastructure could lead to both the revival of the inner city and protection of our natural ecology."[4]

In 2001, Ryan sent his plan and other relevant materials to various people who he thought would be key stakeholders, including the Metropolitan Atlanta Rapid Transit Authority (MARTA), the governor, and the mayor. Momentum grew and they were invited to host a public meeting to describe the vision. Subsequently, over the next several years and through different roles, including working for the city, private firms, and now his own consulting practice, Ryan kept engaging with officials and the community. The BeltLine officially opened in 2008, but it's still very much a work in process.

The BeltLine is ambitious. Arguably the largest urban economic development project in the United States at the moment, between 2005 and 2019 the BeltLine attracted approximately $500 million in direct investment and over $5 billion in private investment. At its core, the BeltLine is today essentially a long pedestrian throughway that leverages the old railway tracks, not dissimilar to one of Gravel's inspirations: the smaller-scale Promenade Plantée in Paris. Around that thoroughfare, neighborhoods are coming back to life and private real estate investment is pouring in. Many of the adjacent neighborhoods have increased total jobs (between 2002 and 2017) at rates between 45% and almost 1,000%, according to the BeltLine Data Explorer.

Still, only about half of the envisioned trail system is built out, and Ryan wishes it was happening more quickly. He also wishes that one foundational aspect of the BeltLine vision – the creation of more affordable housing – was more of a shared, consistent priority among all players. One of the concerns from the community has always been that increasing property values would price out original residents of neighborhoods adjacent to the BeltLine. Indeed, the project has had considerable impact on home prices, with several BeltLine neighborhoods experiencing price per-square-foot increases between 2013 and 2018 of more than 100%.[5]

Ryan's frustrations – with the speed of progress, with shifting priorities, with the ever-changing personnel involved – are part of the reason he has had an episodic relationship with the project over the years. In 2016, he went so far as to resign from the board of the Atlanta BeltLine Partnership, the project's fundraising arm. But he has always stayed involved – whether deep in the heart of the planning and execution or influencing from the periphery. Although it may sound like a ridiculous metaphor, it was hard for us not to think of Ryan as a bit of a sheepdog for the project, helping to stave off impending chaos among hundreds of involved parties while ensuring the whole flock keeps on moving forward. According to people who know about these things, sheepdogs work based on two very simple rules: "The first rule: The sheepdog learns how to make the sheep come together in a flock. The second rule: Whenever the sheep are in a tightly knit group, the dog pushes them forwards."[6] And those are exactly the types of things Ryan has been doing for close to 22 years at this point.

One of the unique things about the BeltLine is the degree to which, in the early stages, it garnered widespread support from anyone who heard about the idea. What was particularly unique was that you had factions – who would normally be at odds with each other – each vocally supporting the idea. Community activists agreed with developers, politicians with nonprofits: the idea had broad-based support. In short, Ryan had envisioned something that had considerable and broad-based desirability that, so long as it built and sustained momentum, was destined to cross the "if"-to-"when" chasm. There was nobody who could argue it wasn't a great idea.

That hardly means it was easy.

First, for Ryan to even come up with the idea, he had to eschew a lot of what he had learned in urban planning. To be clear, Ryan isn't trying to disparage his schooling; he simply conceives of his job to be more about design and less about planning. He says:

A lot of people get into urban planning to save the world, and I guess that's what I was also doing. But the profession of planning is usually bureaucratic. I don't mean that in a negative way, but you don't ask the bureaucracy what you should be doing or what the goal is; you ask them *how* to do it. It's more like engineering in that way. Not everyone who thinks about cities is thinking aspirationally. Planning is a perfunctory job – getting people moving around and accomplishing logistical challenges . . . A designer imagines what the future *should* look like. You can't really plan out your life until you understand who you are and who you want to become. And if Atlanta is going to more than double its population in the next 20 years,

we're going to change a lot. The question is: Are we
going to grow up to become some other place, or
will we become the best possible version of Atlanta?

Ryan's natural inclination was to envision the goal. He
envisioned the future – he said he wanted to design the future,
not plan it based on existing processes and procedures. He
wanted to decouple the future, untethering it from existing
reality. He started with human needs and figured out how to
get there.

But this isn't one of those grand stories where the brilliant visionary knows from day one exactly what they want to
achieve. It happened more organically. At his first job after
graduate school, Ryan was working on a project in one of the
neighborhoods along the route of his BeltLine thesis and he
started talking to his co-workers about it. "The more we talked,
the more they were intrigued and I kept answering questions
about it," Ryan remembers. "I wouldn't have really gone out
and shared the idea on my own, but they really loved it . . . the
more people we talked to, the more people wanted to hear it.
So I was kind of compelled to go along for the ride."

Ryan soon met Cathy Woolard, who would become a city
council representative for District Six. Woolard was particularly interested in the transit component of the concept. When
she was elected city council president, she pushed for town hall
meetings on the idea in her district. Woolard became an important champion of the idea and her staff supported Ryan and a
few other volunteers.

It took several years of many meetings a week to create
the groundswell of support that the idea garnered. Any objections that were raised weren't about the vision of the project;
they were about who the project was for, and whether it would

be built. And to launch a project of this magnitude, you really need broad-based support. Ryan's role was to answer questions about what it might mean for communities, sometimes delving deep into the minutiae. People wanted to figure out where their house was relative to the plans, seeking to envision what their lives would be like once the project got underway.

One of the beautiful things about the design was that it mostly leveraged abandoned land around the rail lines, at that time a breeding ground for crime. It didn't rip through neighborhoods or disrupt existing infrastructure. Ryan told us, "It wasn't scary to anyone because it was at the industrial edge of the neighborhood." Ryan used his nights, weekends, and vacation time to volunteer to continue to meet interested parties, designing apartments by day and out in the community by night engaging with church groups, business groups, neighborhood groups, city council – anyone who wanted to hear about it.

Eventually, enough people did hear about it. And advocates for different issues all saw something in the project: "Advocates for housing, bicycling, pedestrians, transit, tree canopy protection, parks, water, all saw their issue in this. And it wasn't just the white hipster set most associated with gentrification – it was everyone." One seminal moment came in 2003, at a meeting of the Atlanta Regional Commission – the group responsible for allocating regional share of transportation funding. The team called on their broad coalition to attend the meeting:

> We sent out an email to get people to go to that meeting and advocate for the BeltLine to be on the list. We weren't asking for it to be at the top of the list; we just wanted to be on the list. This is the kind of meeting where you might find one or two citizens attending – mostly gadfly types. We flooded that room with 100 people. And I was there, as a sort of spokesperson for the details of the idea.

Initially, Ryan was nervous about making a public comment on the record. But his nerves were at least partially settled when he heard two women whom he didn't know talking about the project before the meeting started:

> I was standing behind these two women, and I heard them saying that "our project is this 22-mile loop. . . our project connects 45 neighborhoods," and so on. They were talking about *our* project. I recognized in that moment the power of the public believing in and taking ownership of the idea was what was going to make it happen. They would empower and ultimately obligate their representatives to follow through on the vision . . . the public really wanted it and they were going to vote based on your support

of it. As an elected official, if you didn't support it, you weren't going to make it.

This was the signal; Gravel knew they were moving through the "if"-to-"when" phase change. The broad basis of support combined with willingness of others to take personal, individual ownership of the project compelled him to shift his stance and the way he was provoking the future.

Whether they knew it or not, Ryan, Woolard, and the broader team quickly began leaning on almost every mode of "when" provocation to keep up momentum. Sometimes they were in drive mode, achieving small wins as they transformed abandoned land into park and playground space. At other times, they could do nothing more than activate a broad coalition to achieve more complex subgoals – the passage of a piece of legislation or approval of a budget. In an era before social media, they got people doing things like writing letters to editors, calling council representatives, attending meetings with talking points, and so on. Although the long arc of Ryan's story paints him as the very definition of an Adapt provocateur, that doesn't mean that has been his only mode of action. He had to use them all.

The BeltLine project naturally went through a number of growing pains as it got off the ground, and those growing pains have continued to this day. Ryan has been in and out over time as leadership has evolved. But the idea has enough momentum that it continues to flourish. The Atlanta BeltLine organization still has as lofty a set of goals as Ryan ever had. It may not be everything that Ryan had originally envisioned, brought to life in exactly the way he would have liked, but it's certainly a reasonable facsimile.

And whether as sheepdog, conscience, visionary, or just another volunteer, Ryan has been involved at every step of the way. It occurred to us that he seems to have *The Godfather*'s Michael Corleone syndrome: "Just when I thought I was out, they pull me back in." Although he has been mostly working on his own for the last decade or so, he's never been fully "out." Humorously, on one of the days we interviewed him, he claimed to not be involved with the project, and then said that he was "just on the phone with leadership the other day."

Ryan's ability as an Adapt provocateur has been that, while he claims to have some strong ideas about the BeltLine as it relates to the things that make a difference between its working and not working, he recognizes that the nature of city development requires others to build on his original vision. He has the ability to take himself out of the picture to allow others to evaluate the strength of the idea, not his role in it. As a result, the BeltLine has adapted and morphed over time – and will continue to do so – with the citizenry of Atlanta taking ownership of the ideas and building on it.

Part of the allure of the BeltLine – and one of the things that naturally enabled it to pass the desirability and viability hurdles – is that it isn't just one thing. "It is a community revitalization project," Ryan notes, "an economic development project, a transit project, a trail project, a greenway project, a public health project, a public art project, a public park project, a water quality project. It is a brownfield remediation project. It is all kinds of things, so whatever your interest is, you can see yourself in it." The best way to understand the impact of the BeltLine is to listen to Atlanta residents talk about it. They use terms like "godsend" and "brilliant," noting that people get out and walk to places they never would before. The way of living in a city that Ryan experienced in Paris 25 years ago is coming to life for Atlantans: humans connecting with humans across social boundaries in a way that just hasn't been a reality before.

Some of our favorite anecdotes from Ryan relate to the organic nature of life on the BeltLine. In one, he relayed the experience of walking home from work and unexpectedly crossing paths with his daughter riding her bike home from school. It sounds like a simple, unremarkable scene, until you consider that the scene would literally not have been possible without the BeltLine. Ryan would be stuck in his car passing the nameless, faceless thousands on his way to work, missing out on the happy accident of a brief interaction with his child on a bike. As the BeltLine comes further to life, innovations small and large will blossom, driven by others working on the platform that Ryan provoked. And he'll be there to experience it with them, quietly relishing their successes:

> A local artist had an idea for a lantern parade. She said people would participate by making their own homemade lanterns and walking down the trail in the dark. The first year, about 200 people participated, the next year there were 400, then 800, then 1,200, then 12,000. And now, more than 80,000 people each year are making homemade lanterns for this event. It's ridiculously beautiful. And it all happened because of a simple slab of concrete. That really gets me.

CHAPTER 12

Valerie Irick Rainford

Steve first had the chance to hear Valerie Rainford speak in February 2020 during a talk focused on the support of Black talent. She was direct and uncompromising but did not lecture. She had a warmth and genuineness about her, but when it came to her point of view, she did not flinch. Valerie shared how she thought about the people she encountered over the years in the organizations where she drove change. She had a simple framework like a stoplight chart, categorizing people into reds, yellows, and greens. When Valerie introduced her framework, Steve immediately thought he fell into the green category. He had always thought of himself as a champion of diversity. He frequently pointed to the fact that his team was 50% women, and he was proud of the fact that he had been associated with the success of several women mentees over the years.

Valerie started with the reds and the description was what Steve expected: the people who directly block progress in an organization. She then described the greens, and that was also what he expected: the people who take positive action for Black colleagues.[1] But there was a twist. You couldn't be a green without data-based evidence that your actions had impact. Could you actually point to an increase in something of importance among your Black colleagues? If you couldn't, you were a yellow: someone who isn't standing in the way deliberately but who is part of a large swath of people whose actions haven't created any discernable impact.

As Steve thought about the organization that had been under his direct control for the last five years, he couldn't point to any data that would have made him green. It was an important moment. Valerie had very simply moved Steve's mental goal posts in a meaningful way.

Valerie has had this kind of impact wherever she has been in her career. She is a serial provocateur. Her impact has been felt by the organizations she's been a part of and, more importantly, by the people with whom she's worked. Following graduation from Fordham, she launched her career at the Federal Reserve Bank of New York where she started as a bank examiner – and one of the first women on a team of men who expected that the women would make the coffee – and ended up becoming a senior vice president and the first Black woman to run corporate real estate. Valerie then moved to JPMorgan Chase where, after a number of successful senior positions, she was charged with leading the company's efforts to advance Black talent at all levels in the organization. Subsequently, she founded Elloree Talent Strategies – risking a steady and consistent salary to go out on her own – and found immediate success in garnering clients. She now counts 16 CEOs as her clients (mostly white men, by the way) and has effectively doubled her income in the first year of operation. And this success was achieved before the murder of George Floyd greatly stimulated demand among executive leadership for advancement strategies for Black talent.

Throughout her career, Valerie has been known as the fixer. She earned a reputation as the person you throw into a so-called burning building to put out the fire. She built this reputation at the Federal Reserve, working her way through

a variety of roles over her 21-year career there. It was that reputation that attracted JPMorgan Chase to recruit her and create a role for her working on projects across the company.

When we were putting together our initial list of potential provocateurs for these last few chapters, we were unaware of Valerie's personal backstory. We had been introduced to her through her work with Deloitte (full disclosure, Deloitte is one of Valerie's clients as we work on advancing diverse talent in our own organization). We were impressed with her professional accomplishments and wanted to understand more about *how* she drove the change she did at JPMorgan Chase, the Fed, and elsewhere. When we met with her on Zoom for the first time and started to understand what she overcame in her early years, we were both floored and awed.

To say the odds were stacked against Valerie would be a monumental understatement. When you pair her professional accomplishments with what she's dealt with in her personal life, you might say what she's achieved is nothing short of miraculous. It's impossible to do Valerie's professional story justice without sharing some of her personal backstory. That said, the two of us feel a bit sheepish providing a relatively short and antiseptic telling of her story, which deserves more of your time and emotional connection. We highly recommend that you read Valerie's words about the critical moments that shaped her life in her short autobiography *Until the Brighter Tomorrow: One Woman's Courageous Climb from the Projects to the Podium*.

Valerie's upbringing was characterized by hardship and pain, but also intense love and devotion among her family members. Valerie's great grandparents were slaves and her grandparents were sharecroppers. Her mother and father were raised on neighboring rural farms in South Carolina in the 1930s. They each completed a sixth-grade education, and her grandmother never had an education. Valerie's mom was one of six children. When her mom was three, Valerie's grandfather was murdered – run off the road under suspicious circumstances that some in the family believe may have been a hate crime, never solved, with his killers never brought to justice. Three days after the killing, the family for whom Valerie's mom's family was farming essentially put them out. Valerie said,

> That killing set the trajectory for our family to this day. Because my grandfather is now dead and my grandmother has all these little babies . . . The family that they were farming for put locks on the barn preventing my grandmother from continuing to sharecrop the farm. My grandmothers' children were split amongst family members so she could find work. My grandmother, at some point in the future as part of Roosevelt's New Deal, cleaned houses and planted trees for government income. To

this day I drive along the roads of South Carolina wondering which trees my grandmother planted.

The children were divided among family members in an effort to make ends meet.

Valerie's oldest uncle, "Junior," carried a heavy burden to help his mother, often stealing chickens to help feed the family (he was 16 at the time). Valerie's mom, split from her siblings who were being raised by different parts of the family, hated picking cotton and was looking for any way to get out. At 18, she married Valerie's father. Eventually, they moved to Columbia, South Carolina, where they would struggle. "She was so tired of picking cotton," Valerie said. "She used to joke that she would interrupt with 'get married' to the first guy who said 'let's.'"

Valerie's mom worked two jobs and cleaned houses, and her father drove a truck. Her oldest brother, Jay, was born in 1947, and her middle brother, Anthony ("Ankie"), was born in 1953. Valerie joined the family in 1964, soon after which Jay shipped off to Vietnam. A few years later, when she was three, Valerie's parents split. They each decided to migrate north, as did many Black Americans in the 1960s, in search of better opportunities. They relocated to areas close to other siblings in New York (her mom) and Connecticut (her father). With both parents needing to work full time, and with her older brother just getting settled back from Vietnam and her middle brother starting his own family, Valerie was left in South Carolina to be raised by the Rivers family, a choice all-too-similar to the choice her grandmother was forced to make. She was "the fifth daughter" in their family of four girls.

For periods of time, Valerie would reunite and live in New York with her mom, who was attempting to make a go at working multiple jobs and raising a daughter. Valerie's mom eventually remarried a man named Moses who was abusive. On one evening when Valerie was visiting, Moses got drunk and hit Valerie's mom on the head with a beer bottle. Luckily, Valerie, then a first grader, was able to call her uncle to intervene; otherwise, she suspects her mom would have died that evening. On the heels of that experience, Valerie was shipped back to South Carolina to complete second grade with the Rivers family.

Over the next several years, Valerie was shuttled back and forth from South Carolina to New York. Her mom desperately tried to improve their situation at every juncture, even if only incrementally. Valerie recalls, "We were still moving homes every year. I remember the place we were living in in fifth grade. It backed up against a swamp and there were these rats that were literally the size of cats. She was always just trying to find something better. One house didn't have heat; this one had rats. Another had a landlord who sexually harassed her. So I was in a different school every year."

Valerie's mom was her first role model for being a provocateur. Never accepting her trajectory as it was presented to her, Valerie's mom taught her the value of persistence and of never accepting your circumstances as a given, even if the moves available to you are limited. If you don't do something, nobody else will do it for you.

As Valerie reflects on what her mom taught her, she states, "A lot of people would say 'woe is me, woe is me,' but I just look at what my mom was trying to do and all I see is that she was constantly trying to make things better, which is important to how I think today. I'm never going to settle on something that doesn't work for me. I'm always going to be looking for something that's better than what I currently have. I learned this from my mother and all of her sixth-grade education and three jobs. That's what she taught me."

Following her mom's example, Valerie didn't accept her surroundings as given. As she approached high school, she was zoned to attend a school known among kids as the "neighborhood drugstore." Fearing she would end up like many kids at that school, she researched others she could attend, including a few different Catholic schools; she was not at all deterred by the fact that she was not Catholic – as she says, "I saw these people in these schools and their situation seemed to be much different than my situation." At the same time, Valerie was working as a cashier in a supermarket, trying to help her mom keep up with their bills. Determined to attend a better school, Valerie offered to help pay a portion of the $250 per month tuition to enroll at St. Catherine's Academy in the Bronx.

We asked Valerie how she discovered St. Catherine's. She replied, "The phone book. I was looking at high schools. I was just desperate to not be in the situation where my best friend had gotten pregnant. I didn't want to attend 'the neighborhood drugstore.' One time, my mom caught me smoking – one time! – and she beat the bejeezus out of me. I couldn't go to that school that would put me in these situations frequently. I couldn't disappoint my mom."

During high school, Valerie continued to work at the supermarket to pay for her education. Facile with numbers – "in those days, you actually had to add it up" – she became known as the fastest checkout clerk in the supermarket and customers loved to come through her line. She worked her way up to be the supermarket's night bookkeeper, with her mom picking her up late at night and dropping her off at home before heading to her own overnight job. Valerie's skill was noticed by one of the supermarket customers, who offered her a job at a nearby bank. It was there that, like Ryan in Paris, she watched others and learned a valuable life lesson that enabled her transition from JPMorgan Chase to

founding Elloree Talent. She learned the power of saving. As
she notes,

> I saw these people coming through the checkout
> line in the supermarket wearing the same clothes all
> the time, using multiple cat food coupons. I used to
> wonder with my mom whether they were eating the
> cat food. But when I got to the bank, the same peo-
> ple would come in with their passbooks and they
> had six-figure dollar amounts in their accounts. I'm
> like, wait: they aren't eating the cat food; they're just
> saving their money.

Valerie was using the critical provocateur's tool of observing others throughout her life. She thinks her strength of
observation stems from the constant changes she faced and her
need to consistently look for something that might go wrong
or how things could be a bit better. Valerie said,

> I used to visit my grandmother and she would tell
> me stories. You'd drive into town and you'd cross the
> railroad tracks, and it's mostly white people, and the
> other side of the tracks it's mostly black people.
> That's what I saw as a kid. I was constantly trying to
> figure out: Why are things better over there than
> over here? And why can't I do the thing over there?
> That's kind of how my brain is wired. How come I
> can't do that thing? It was curiosity, not militance.
> Or, if these kids drive their own cars at 16 and I'm
> taking a bus, how might life be different?

It was during Valerie's sophomore year at St Catherine's
Academy, the school she was attending specifically to avoid
falling into the traps she associated with the other schools,

when she was doing homework in the wee hours of the night after work, that Ankie, her middle brother, committed suicide after his own set of tragedies. Valerie said, "I mean, it just rocked our family, no notice or warning whatsoever. He just could never get a good job or anything right. It was just so hard on him . . . my mom was really never the same. She was the same in that she kept working and hustling to make things better but, at any moment, she would just cry."

In the wake of Ankie's suicide, Valerie changed her college plans. She had wanted to go back to South Carolina but decided that her mom was not ready for her to leave. She decided to attend Fordham University, which allowed her to continue working at the bank, attend school, and be there for her mom. During Valerie's freshman year, while in the university gymnasium watching a basketball game, she met "a guy," Tony. They fell in love and were married in August the following year, before her sophomore year began.

A month after the wedding, Valerie's mom took her own life. Valerie said, "I was devastated. I thought it was my fault. I left her alone a month before to get married to this guy. So, I blamed it all on him. I blamed myself. I blamed it on everybody. What was I thinking by falling in love with this dude?"

Valerie decided to take a break from Fordham to spend time with Tony, who supported her. She also spent more time with her maternal grandmother, who had lost her husband, separated her children, struggled throughout her life to build her family, and then lost her daughter to suicide. "I would just get on a bus and go see her," Valerie said. "I'd never seen her cry. After all the things she'd been through, I had never seen her cry. She said to me 'I think she just forgot, Val . . . she forgot all the things I tried to teach her, like that God don't give you more than you can bear. She just forgot to hang in there.'"

Following that trip to see her grandmother, Valerie re-enrolled at Fordham. She reports that she has "been on a mission ever since. I can still hear my mother saying, 'You can do this, you can do this,' and my grandmother saying, 'Don't forget.'"

When she re-enrolled, Valerie wanted to complete her studies at Fordham as quickly as possible so that she could graduate on schedule. She sat with her counselor and decided the best path to do so was to switch from premed to economics. It was in an economics class that she first learned about the Federal Reserve. Later, she noticed they were coming to campus and signed up to be interviewed with a woman she still knows today, Renee Ragin. Valerie was still working at the bank, and that day, as she rushed to get from work to the interview, it was pouring rain. Anyone who has ever tried to get from point A to point B in New York City during a rainstorm can empathize with what Valerie must have looked and felt like coming into that interview. In her words, "a hot mess."

As she tried to compose herself in the bathroom before the interview, she ran into an empathetic stranger who helped reassure a visibly upset Valerie. The stranger told Valerie, "Honey, you're going to be okay."

That stranger turned out to be Renee Ragin.

Not only did Valerie pull it together, she nailed the interview. Afterward Renee said, "I told you it was going to be okay."

Valerie's first choice of where to start her career was open market operations but, since they didn't hire directly from Fordham University, she started in banking examinations. In our interview, Valerie made sure to point out, with a grin, "I wound up running the open market operations discount window when I was at the Fed."

Although Valerie was now in the professional world, life didn't get much easier. She was assigned to a group with another woman from Fordham, Patricia. Patricia and Valerie were the first two women in the group. Valerie was also the first Black person on the team. Other team members – white men – made it clear that Patricia and Valerie weren't wanted on the team, asking them to perform demeaning tasks like lugging large suitcase-sized files from across downtown Manhattan and fetching coffee – this in addition to the sexual harassment. It was bad enough that Patricia quit on the fourth day. But Valerie needed the job – she couldn't quit – and she wasn't going to forget the advice of her grandmother and her mom.

One day, several weeks in, Valerie was accused by one of her senior co-workers of bringing him the wrong papers from the office. At her wits' end, Valerie told him to "get your own damn papers" and stormed out.

After she spoke up, they started treating her differently. One co-worker in particular started asking Valerie for her point of view during meetings, a subtle show of support. Within 18 months, she was named supervising examiner. She notes, "Some of my biggest supporters came out of that room, with those guys who were old enough to be my father, who treated me with huge disrespect in the beginning."

Early on, Valerie was invited to a manager training and development luncheon for high-potential employees, and she leveraged it to launch an uncommon career path at the Fed. She met senior leaders and started asking questions – lots of them. People noticed her curiosity and her career accelerated. She had 14 different roles in 21 years. She developed a reputation as a problem solver, a fixer, someone who could be dropped into a mess with instructions to "fix it." Whether it was fixing the backlog of accounting items in accounting operations, renovating the historic 75-year-old landmark facility and its original generator as head of corporate real estate (despite having zero electrical engineering experience), leading planning for the Y2K crisis (despite the crisis never coming, Valerie assures us, "We were ready"), or, in multiple areas, automating inefficient manual processes like securities transfers and trust receipts ("Seriously," Valerie says, "couriers would come to the Fed to pick up and transport trust receipts"), she skillfully addressed the challenges she was tasked with and worked her way up.

In all these roles, Valerie provoked the organization. She "envisioned" by leveraging data to highlight the challenge and the better way of solving the problem. Knowing – both explicitly and intuitively – that a Black woman couldn't just move *in power* (getting stuff done because she was in charge), Valerie created what we think is her signature approach: get the data on the table to make the problem clear, imagine a better way, and don't assume that any obstacles that appear are insurmountable. After all, Valerie had dealt with a lot worse growing up, so any obstacle she faced in her career paled in comparison. It was with this calm but focused demeanor that she tackled problems over her career at the Fed.

Valerie also employed the provocateur's tool of "Activating." In particular, she became adept at gaining and leveraging the advocacy of senior white men who wanted to drive change. At the Fed, it was Tim Geithner. At JPMorgan Chase, it was Jamie Dimon. Now, it's the 16 CEOs she advises on how to advance diverse talent.

Geithner was the first executive who asked for Valerie's help in addressing the issue of diversity at the Federal Reserve. Valerie attacked the problem, as she had others in her career, by clearly and unemotionally presenting the challenge through data. She, with the support of Geithner, made a successful case for a diversity program, leading to the first chief diversity officer role at the Federal Reserve and the launch of women's groups. Valerie considers this her greatest accomplishment at the Fed.

Geithner, though, refused to make her the chief diversity officer, suggesting instead that she could have more impact as a senior Black business leader than as a diversity officer. Although Valerie was disappointed at first, she later came to see this as a gift. She *was* better off driving diversity as a business leader, and that is essentially what she still does today. The effort at the Fed also taught Valerie the important role that data plays in creating the case for change in the area of diversity.

Data + Supportive Leader + Agent of Change became Valerie's go-to formula for provocation, in particular on a topic that over the years has received a lot of discussion but insufficient action: advancing Black talent in corporate America. Valerie clarified why the supportive leader must be accompanied by an agent of change, who is given freedom to move: "You need the CEO to change cultural norms. And even if they are courageous, they may not have the time or specific skills and knowledge to drive change in the space. And, by the way, the agent of change has to be a business leader, with business knowledge and expertise. That's why most chief diversity officers fail; they are not put in a position to be an agent of change."

In 2007, based on her reputation as a firefighter, Valerie was recruited by JPMorgan Chase to work in the organization of the chief administrative officer (CAO). The CAO's office was integrative across the organization, and the intent was to have Valerie work on a variety of projects and then determine where she fit best. A few days in, Valerie was having second thoughts. The atmosphere didn't feel right. She considered quitting and trying to go back to the Fed. But her husband, Tony, said, "You've never quit anything in your life." That jolted Valerie to decide to bring her authentic self to work.

She decided that she was going to say good morning to literally everyone she interacted with that day: the security guard at the front desk, the gruff cafeteria worker slinging her breakfast, and everyone else within earshot. It helped.

Over the next several years, Valerie worked on some of the most important issues facing JPMorgan Chase through the financial crisis, *following the fire*. Out of one of the challenges she was working on, Valerie identified the need to increase her staff in one of the businesses, and as part of that, made her first case for a diversity strategy. As they ramped up that particular effort, the team increased women, minority, and veteran hires by 30%.

Over time at JPMorgan Chase (JPMC), a number of Valerie's key advocates transitioned out of the company and Valerie, whose career had been enabled by having a senior leader task her against critical issues, was languishing on the sidelines. Valerie decided it was time to either find something or leave. So, she effectively recreated her "good morning" tour, except this time with the JPMC senior executive ranks. She spoke with 42 different executives and was still looking for the next thing at JPMorgan Chase when a fellow Fordham grad suggested she meet with a key member of Jamie Dimon's team with a similar role to the CAO whose team she had initially joined. This leader was initially shocked that Valerie had been lying fallow for any time and helped get her back to firefighting.

In 2016, Valerie learned that Jamie Dimon was determined to do a much better job recruiting, retaining, and promoting Black talent at JPMorgan. Initially, Valerie was skeptical, but she was convinced enough to attend a town hall Dimon was holding in the headquarters lobby. His remarks stunned Valerie:

> For over an hour, he sat and talked – in 2016 – about why he was not happy with where we were as an

organization around advancing Black talent. He shared that what he learned running any other business was that somebody has to be responsible for it. For over an hour, he talked about setting up this 'Black segment initiative' – that's what he was calling it – to advance Black talent. No specifics yet. With over 200,000 people watching; they were spellbound. I thought, who sits in the lobby and talks about Black people for over an hour. . .and stays for another hour answering questions live?

Valerie mentioned she'd be willing to help if Dimon was interested and, sure enough, later that afternoon her phone rang and she was asked to throw her hat in the ring to be the one responsible for driving the "Black segment initiative." After a series of conversations with senior leaders, she met with Dimon and the conversation went well. But Valerie was concerned about an "insignificant" point: the name. "It seems limiting. Initiatives start and stop. But I do love it when you say 'advancing Black leaders.'" Jamie looked at Valerie and said, "I don't actually care what you call it. Just f---ing fix it."

Valerie was charged to come back to Dimon with a plan in 30 days, which was reduced to 20 days. She pulled out her playbook and assembled the data. She created a directory of over 100 Black executives from outside the company who had had some conversations with JPMorgan, with recommendations on who JPMorgan should hire right away.

With her data and her list, Valerie had burst the myth that you couldn't find Black talent. Dimon, recognizing this, immediately brought Valerie to the operating committee with him for an unscheduled discussion. Valerie was prepared; it just so happened that she had made the exact number of copies as there were people on the operating committee. They hired 5 Black senior executives out of that book over the next 90 days.

Valerie was given an unencumbered budget and asked to make more happen.

Valerie notes, "I was the messenger, leader, owner, pushing out information. Leaders would invite me to their leadership team meetings and talk about what they should do next. I always started with studying their data."

JPMorgan Chase's progress under Valerie's leadership was remarkable. The company reported on progress each year to shareholders – a step that itself would be progress for many companies. In 2019, three years into the program, JPMorgan Chase reported in a shareholder letter, "Since 2016, the firm has increased the number of Black MDs [managing directors] by 41% and Black EDs [executive directors] by 53%." Valerie's work also led to the creation of a sister strategy, Advancing Black Pathways, which focused on homeownership, wealth creation, and financial literacy. Valerie's success was buoyed further by a sense of pride. Valerie recounted, "The company is all jazzed up. People are coming in. They are getting promoted. Every time someone gets elevated we announced them to the entire Black community. Jamie had asked me in the initial conversation to coalesce the Black community and it felt good."

JPMorgan Chase also asked Valerie to talk to clients to share learnings so they could take similar steps. Therein lay the seeds for Valerie's next move. Leveraging the provocateur's tool of observation, she saw a latent interest from executives to replicate the success of JPMorgan Chase. They just didn't know what to do. Valerie had several requests from CEOs of JPMorgan Chase clients asking to "loan her out." And Valerie reminds us in this moment – "those were all white men, you know."

This caused Valerie to think about how she might shape the world around her further, beyond the impact she had at the Fed and JPMorgan. Having spoken to all those CEOs, she was confident that she could provoke a latent energy for organizations to more productively advance diverse talent, leveraging both the data and Valerie as an agent of change. Despite having a comfortable job and decades of productive work ahead, after having come from the most challenging of circumstances, Valerie decided to risk it all and start her own organization to help companies. She saw that this as a space and place to intervene had shifted from "if" to "when."

As she reflected on her logic, she said, "I've got these CEOs in my ear and I think there's a win here. I think there are organizations out there that want to follow JPMorgan Chase's lead. And I want to help more organizations. I've done enough for you guys to keep it going . . . but I don't think they're done with me."

Valerie successfully pitched JPMorgan Chase to become the first client of Elloree Talent Strategies, named for the South Carolina town she came from. Valerie is now out on her own.

Her strategy and approach are clearly grounded in her experiences. Data + Supportive Leader + Agent of Change. She will only work for chief executives. She's learned that if you don't have the CEOs on board, you won't get very far. No exceptions. That's a risk – greatly reducing her potential addressable market – where she now has a payroll to make.

So far, it hasn't been a problem. As mentioned, Valerie now serves 16 CEOs. On Dimon's advice, she is structuring only short engagements: "Get in and get out" was his advice to her when she was launching Elloree Talent. Contracts are no longer than 16 weeks. Valerie insists that Elloree access data to inform where clients should focus, both demonstrating the problem and showcasing the solution through the numbers. Although she might sign companies up for a longer journey given the length of time it takes to really transform, Valerie wants organizations to own the commitment. If they don't, there are better places to focus her time and effort.

As she said, "If you want me to help you build the strategy, I'd be willing to do that. If you want me to coach talent, I can do that. But on the initial engagement, where we look at the data, it has to be with the CEO. And it has to include unfettered access to your data so we can look at the opportunities you have."

Valerie's insight into her community of clients has been profound. She sees a group of leaders who legitimately want to help advance diverse talent. In their minds, they feel that they *are* acting, but the data doesn't show it. They're yellow, not green. So Valerie is there to act as an agent of change to help them recognize the gap to their desired outcomes and the root causes shaping the status quo.

How has this played out for Valerie? On the day she left JPMorgan Chase, her LinkedIn announcement touched a quarter million people. Then the phone started ringing. Now? Good luck getting hold of her because she is sold out. At the time of writing, seven large companies are on big data engagements, touching over half a million employees, and there's a strong pipeline for more. She is a coach to dozens of senior executives. And if you think this is just a case of being in the right place at the right time, as corporate America became "woke" after the murder of George Floyd: nope. She was successful before the summer of 2020, having already predicted that this "if" would be a "when." So, yes, she benefits from the incremental demand, but it's because she was positioned as the leader in this field well before the surge.

Her focus now, in her speaking and her work, is to get companies to expand their frame from diversity and inclusion to diversity, *equity*, and inclusion. Valerie, however, says the focus on diversity and inclusion is important, but not enough:

"You can have a D&I program but still have inequitable outcomes. If you look at the data and you've only got 2% of your leadership team who are Black or Latinx, that's an inequitable outcome. It's not enough to just assume that because you have a diversity and inclusion program, it's working. If you're not bringing up whole swaths of people, you're still leading in an inequitable environment. A large part of the reason we are in this situation is that people haven't been taught the history of the country in a way where people understand the inequities. Focusing on equity, looking at the data – that helps make leaders accountable."

One of Valerie's first clients at Elloree perfectly summed up her role as a provocateur: "I've never seen anything so factual and actionable. It is because you are a truth teller." Valerie wants to be remembered for this: "There are plenty of diversity and leadership consultants out there. I want to be known as a truth teller who drives impact."

CONCLUSION: MINIMALLY VIABLE THOUGHTS

In the spirit of any two data points connecting to create a trend line, we thought we'd end *Provoke* in the same way we ended *Detonate*: with some "minimally viable thoughts." These are ideas that might have been on the cutting-room floor, or notions we've been pondering that were not sufficiently formed to merit inclusion elsewhere. Our aspiration in sharing these ideas is to provoke conversation among our readers in the hopes they can be improved or alternatively discarded as "ifs" that will never become "whens."

ON THE IMPORTANCE OF FUN

While we were writing this book, our editor, Tim Sullivan, observed that "it's clear that you both (and many of the people in the stories) have fun." When we asked him why that was noteworthy, he responded: "Intellectual play is important. I would think that writing scenarios to play with is in fact fun, in addition to being hard work. In a group exercise, envisioning possible futures has got to be a blast. But I would guess that in many settings there's an awful lot of self-seriousness."

He is 100% right. There is an awful lot of self-seriousness out there and, in our opinion, not enough levity. Almost all organizations – especially scaled, successful ones that have a reputation to uphold – take themselves at least a little too seriously. Of course, many are doing (very) important work. But there is no law that says that doing important work has to be done by people who aren't having fun doing it or that the work can't be made to be more fun in some way. The two of us are lucky to have found jobs and roles in which we (mostly) have fun doing what we do, and that's why we stay. This entire book was written without a single in-person meeting, but we still had a good time.

However, we wondered: Does this matter to the outcome? Do teams that have fun together create better outcomes? We haven't studied this nor have we researched it extensively to determine if it has been proven elsewhere but we just haven't seen it. But our hypothesis is that teams that have fun are better at provoking for a better future. Here's our logic.

If a team is having fun, it is almost always due to a foundation of mutual trust and respect and the individuals on the team feel more comfortable sharing ideas off the cuff – tossing them out there before they are fully formed and actively seeking for others to build on and improve them. On teams that don't have fun, it's quite the opposite. If the lack of fun is due to mistrust or dislike of one another, then the lack of sharing may simply be an act of spite. If it is due to discomfort with one another, then fear of embarrassment may keep team members shuttered. And if the lack of fun is due to the meeting simply being excruciating in the way it is being run, then the lack of sharing may be linked to a desperate attempt, at all costs, to just let the thing end. As we discussed earlier in the book, organizational peripheral vision is enhanced by gaining a more expansive look at the real-world "data pool," and that's just not possible if people are shutting down and layering self-imposed blinders over the ones that are naturally caused by "fatal flaws." Fun can have a self-reinforcing multiplier effect as well: if you have fun with people who are different from you, that might just make you more likely to put yourself in more situations with people who are different from you.

The challenge with fun is that it's definitely in the eye of the beholder. What one person might find fun might be a nightmare for another. And there's no doubt that the most "cringe-worthy" fun is forced fun. It's not a matter of running "rah-rah" team-building activities. And it's not a matter of creating social activities for people to get to know one another. Both of these can be valuable but for different purposes. This is about actually having fun doing the work.

We're pretty sure that the only authentic way to catalyze fun in a heterogeneous group is to make it discussable at the outset. It could be as simple as, "We've got some important work to do here and we're simply not going to be better than average unless we make it fun. How do you think we can have fun?" At a minimum, with that simple question, people may feel just a bit more valued and engaged. Once you have even just a modicum of fun, let it build on its own momentum. And definitely skip the "fun meter" surveys. Just count the smiles.

LOOKING AT DATA WITHOUT CONTEXT

In the course of researching *Provoke*, our conversation with Scott E. Page was in fact lots of fun. We think we might have set a record for the most words spoken in an hour meeting; ideas were flying back and forth. In one exchange, Scott shared that he and a number of colleagues were working on some thinking about the role that context plays in understanding data – that is, whether there was value in looking at data without context. Among other things, Scott was looking at the role different factors play in predictions: predictions from the data alone, predictions from context around the data, predictions from marginal changes (i.e., derivatives of the data), and predictions of qualitative changes. His hypothesis is that the skillset to understand marginal effects is different from, say, the skillset to understand qualitative effects.

The investigation seemed fascinating to us and we look forward to seeing the results.

It did get us wondering about a different application of looking at data without context. What if we use that exercise as a mechanism to provoke unexpected action when there appears to be reticence? For example, if market share has been steadily declining for a brand, a typical set of reactions might be to drop price, or to "sex up" the brand, or to add functionality. What if, instead, you take the data series that shows the trend and "blind" it. Put the unmarked data set in front of a team, ask them to imagine the range of different outcomes that might follow, and then ask them to imagine what would need to be true for each outcome to occur. Then, unblind the data and ask the team to tell a story – now with context – about how each thing that would need to be true came to pass. Alternatively, taking learning from Valerie Rainford as she discussed using data about different diverse populations within organizations, ask how this data will move without meaningful intervention.

We're going to try this one ourselves a few times to see whether it works. It could be genius. Or it could be experienced by the teams we work with as a cheap trick.

ON THE VALUE OF RECOGNIZING RECURSION

For many years, Steve and Geoff have both been encouraging all clients who will listen to them that good strategy is about making choices. That's still true and will be for as long as either can imagine. But making a choice is increasingly no more than table stakes. What really matters now – in terms of what will create advantage in a world of uncertainty – is the ability to recognize (and create the management systems to support) the recursive nature of strategic choices and to actively work that recursion. Gone are the days when you could make a series of choices and put them on the shelf until next year's strategic planning process, focusing only on execution in the meantime. Now, every leader needs to be ready to act in ways both big and small on an ongoing basis, to change course or confirm the current heading as external indicators and operational realities reveal themselves.

This idea has echoes of the value of "tinkering" that we wrote about in *Detonate*, introduced to us first by John Seely Brown. Small, continuous, targeted changes on a solid foundation will ultimately beat overhaul of a going concern. The notion of dynamic strategy, in which all choices are up for debate all the time, is a bridge too far. Recursive strategy instead values the constancy of a strategy-in-use while being on the lookout for adjustments in response to unanticipated signals. Critically, it recognizes and plans for the knock-on effects of a shift in choice to the rest of the system. The ability to be agile is only as valuable as the embedded foresight around the pattern of falling dominoes that results.

CEO AS THE LEAD SYSTEM DESIGNER

In Chapter 4, we introduced the "dumb principal" problem, as coined by Richard Thaler – the notion that there often is mis-alignment between the outcomes that an organizational leader wants and the way the members of her team perceive what will best advance their careers.

Perhaps the best way to create positive change in any organization is to align individual incentives with an organizational vision and set of operating principles that are geared to thrive in the face of uncertainty. And as organizations become more and more complex, the CEO becomes increasingly unique in their ability to ensure that behavior is consistent with the desired objectives. CEOs are the only ones with sufficient purview and authority to make sure that what they want to have happen is in fact happening. So why is it that there seems to be an inverse correlation between scale and locus of focus? Typically (again, unscientific), the bigger and more prominent a company becomes, the more its CEO feels the need to look outward and to become the face of the company. What if we encouraged the opposite? What if the more successful we become, the more the CEO turns inward to pay attention to the evermore complex details of the management systems in place to ensure alignment? That might even lead to a shift in the capabilities prized in the C-suite, where the objective function is not just to enhance a reputation and keep the shareholders happy, but also to enhance the collective human experience . . . and maybe even lead to a bit more fun.

We hope with *Provoke* that we've convinced you that action, in some ways, is nearly always superior to inaction because action provides more immediate, more valuable feedback. We also hope that we've left you with a few concepts that can help you identify happenings in your own organization that contribute to systematic blindness – to trends, to phase changes, and to the diverse views of others. You may not find it practical to provoke in all the ways we've described, but our hope is that there is at least one thing that will work given your particular circumstances. Just recognizing the predictable patterns may be enough to prevent inaction.

We also hope that the stories of Debbie, Ryan, and Valerie left you inspired that provocateurs can come from anywhere, from any point of view, and with very different styles.

Tell us what you think. Tweet us @steven_goldbach and @geofftuff. As with *Detonate*, this is meant to be a conversation starter. We would love to hear about what worked, what didn't, and what you wish we could all explore a bit further.

But whether you're the one in charge or the newest member of a team, we genuinely believe that we will all live in a better world if you just go out and DO SOMETHING!

Notes

Chapter 1: Patterns from the Past

1. Christopher McFadden, "The Fascinating History of Netflix," *Interesting Engineering*, July 4, 2020, https://interestingengineering.com/the-fascinating-history-of-netflix.
2. Arnold Zwicky, "Just between Dr. Language and I," *Language Log*, August 7, 2005, http://itre.cis.upenn.edu/~myl/languagelog/archives/002386.html.
3. For more on the "winner take all" economy, see Roger Martin, *When More Is Not Better* (Boston: Harvard Business Review Press, 2020).

Chapter 2: On the Importance of "If" versus "When"

1. Ray Rivera, "Summerville Police Department Hands Out Roll of Toilet Paper Instead of Tickets," *Live 5, WCSC*, March 19, 2020, https://www.live5news.com/2020/03/20/summerville-police-department-handing-out-toilet-paper-instead-tickets/.
2. On consumer habits, see A. G. Lafley and Roger L. Martin, "Customer Loyalty Is Overrated: A Theory of Cumulative Advantage," *Harvard Business Review*, January–February 2017.
3. Brittany Frater, "It Took a Pandemic, but the US Is Finally Discovering the Bidet's Brilliance," *The Guardian*, April 14, 2020, https://www.theguardian.com/us-news/2020/apr/14/us-bidet-toilet-paper-sales-coronavirus; Maria Teresa Hart, "The Bidet's Revival," *The Atlantic*, March 18, 2018, https://www.theatlantic.com/technology/archive/2018/03/the-bidets-revival/555770/; Lisa Boone, "Bidet Sales Spike as Consumers Panic Buy Toilet Paper," *LA Times*, March 16, 2020, https://www.latimes.com/

lifestyle/story/2020-03-16/bidet-sales-spike-as-consumers-panic-buy-toilet-paper.

4. For more on the "Balanced Breakthrough Model," see "What are the three things every idea needs to be successful?" at https://www.ideatovalue.com/inno/nickskillicorn/2019/01/what-are-the-three-things-every-idea-needs-to-be-successful-the-balanced-breakthrough-model/.

5. "Learn the Knowledge of London," *Transport for London*, https://tfl.gov.uk/info-for/taxis-and-private-hire/licensing/learn-the-knowledge-of-london.

6. On e-readers, see Ethan Bronner, "Textbooks Shifting from Printed Page to Screen," *New York Times*, December 1, 1998, https://archive.nytimes.com/www.nytimes.com/library/tech/98/12/biztech/articles/01school-etex.html; Anonymous, "E-Book Timeline," *The Guardian*, January 3, 2002, https://www.theguardian.com/books/2002/jan/03/ebooks.technology; "Ebooks," *Statista*, https://www.statista.com/outlook/213/102/ebooks/europe; Andrew Perrin, "One-in-Five Americans Now Listen to Audiobooks," September 25, 2019, https://www.pewresearch.org/fact-tank/2019/09/25/one-in-five-americans-now-listen-to-audiobooks/.

7. Malcolm Gladwell, *The Tipping Point: How Little Things Can Make a Big Difference* (New York: Little, Brown, 2000).

8. Patricia Cooper, "TRAI Consultation Paper on Roadmap to Promote Broadband Connectivity and Enhanced Broadband Speed," September 21, 2020, https://trai.gov.in/sites/default/files/SpaceX_10112020.pdf.

CHAPTER 3: PERSONAL PATTERNS

1. M. Ross and F. Sicoly, "Egocentric Biases in Availability and Attribution," *Journal of Personality and Social Psychology* 37, no. 3 (1979): 322–336.

2. R. B. Zajonc, "Feeling and Thinking: Preferences Need No Inferences," *American Psychologist* 35, no. 2 (1980): 151–175.

3. S. Eidelman and C. S. Crandall, "A Psychological Advantage for the Status Quo," in J. T. Jost, A. C. Kay, and H. Thorisdottir (Eds.),

Social and Psychological Bases of Ideology and System Justification (New York: Oxford University Press, 1999), pp. 85–105.

4. Gerry Pallier, Rebecca Wilkinson, Vanessa Danthiir, Sabina Kleitman, Goran Knezevic, Lazar Stankov, and Richard D. Roberts, "The Role of Individual Differences in the Accuracy of Confidence Judgments," *The Journal of General Psychology* 129, no. 3 (2002): 257–299.

5. Luigi Mittone and Lucia Savadori, "The Scarcity Bias," *Applied Psychology* 58, no. 3 (July 2009): 453–468.

6. Michael E. Porter and Nitin Nohria, "How CEOs Manage Time," *Harvard Business Review*, July 2018.

CHAPTER 4: EXPANDING PERIPHERAL VISION

1. See, for example, the Kantor Institute's web page on their instruments to assess and evaluate operating systems: https://www .kantorinstitute.com/instruments.

2. See, especially, Scott Page, *The Difference: How the Power of Diversity Creates Better Groups, Firms, Schools, and Societies* (Princeton: Princeton University Press, 2007). Page's website has a wealth of information about his work. Visit https://sites.lsa.umich.edu/ scottepage/research-2/diversity-research/.

3. Google, "Our Hiring Practice," https://careers.google.com/ how-we-hire/.

CHAPTER 5: BIRTH OF A PROVOCATION

1. The following account is drawn from several sources: "Why Was the Attack at Pearl Harbor Such a Surprise?" *Baltimore Sun*, December 1, 1991, https://www.baltimoresun.com/news/bs-xpm-1991-12-01-1991335028; Meg Jones, "Milwaukee's Billy Mitchell Predicted Pearl Harbor Attack," *Milwaukee Journal Sentinel*, December 6, 2006, https://www.jsonline.com/story/news/special-reports/pearl-harbor/2016/12/06/milwaukees-billy-mitchell-predicted-pearl-harbor-attack/91625442/; David A. Pfeiffer, "Sage Prophet or Loose Canon?" *Prologue Magazine* 40, no. 2 (Summer 2008), https://www.archives.gov/publications/prologue/

2008/summer/zacharias.html; "The Radar Warning that Went Unheeded," https://pearlharbor.org/warning-went-unheeded/.

2. Kate Rooney, "Why Jack Dorsey and Other Major Tech Figures Are Suddenly Interested in Africa," CNBC, December 30, 2019, https://www.cnbc.com/2019/12/30/jack-dorsey-follows-tech-companies-investors-in-africa-interest.html.

3. Amanda Stutt, "The Race to Mine Outer Space," Mining.com, May 22, 2020, https://www.mining.com/the-global-race-to-mine-outer-space/.

CHAPTER 6: ENVISION: SEEING THE FUTURE

1. Matthew Teague, "Racing the Storm: The Story of the Mobile Bay Sailing Disaster," *Smithsonian*, July/August 2017, https://www.smithsonianmag.com/history/racing-storm-story-mobile-bay-sailing-disaster-180963686/.

2. Our scenario is built on the Deloitte "Future of Energy" study, which can be accessed at https://www2.deloitte.com/us/en/pages/consulting/articles/energy-scenarios-in-focus.html.

3. You can read the Paris Agreement at https://unfccc.int/process/conferences/pastconferences/paris-climate-change-conference-november-2015/paris-agreement.

CHAPTER 7: POSITION: PREPARING FOR THE CHANGE

1. Our Warby Parker story comes from several sources: Ana Swanson, "Meet the Four-Eyed, Eight-Tentacled Monopoly That Is Making Your Glasses So Expensive," *Forbes*, September 10, 2014, https://www.forbes.com/sites/anaswanson/2014/09/10/meet-the-four-eyed-eight-tentacled-monopoly-that-is-making-your-glasses-so-expensive/#575d088e6b66; Steve Denning, "What's Behind Warby Parker's Success?" *Forbes*, March 23, 2016, https://www.forbes.com/sites/stevedenning/2016/03/23/whats-behind-warby-parkers-success/#e94d221411ac; Katie Perry, "Warby Parker Cut Out the Middleman, Lowering the Price of Glasses Significantly,"

Fox Business, December 20, 2019, https://www.foxbusiness.com/
money/warby-parker-middleman-price-glasses-neil-blumenthal;
Graham Winfrey, "The Mistake That Turned Warby Parker into
an Overnight Legend," *Inc.*, https://www.inc.com/magazine/
201505/graham-winfrey/neil-blumenthal-icons-of-entrepreneur
ship.html; Jordan Crook, "Warby Parker, valued at $3 billion, raises
$245 million in funding," *TechCrunch*, August 27, 2020, https://
techcrunch.com/2020/08/27/warby-parker-valued-
at-3-billion-raises-245-million-in-funding/.
2. Robert Burgelman, Robert Siegel, and Julie Makinen, "Zuora in
2017: Leading the Subscription Economy Revolution," Stanford
Graduate School of Business Case No. SM284 (2018).
3. Michael Grothaus, "A Rediscovered 1997 Video Reveals Why Jeff
Bezos Chose Books and Not CDs to Be Amazon's First Product,"
Fast Company, November 3, 2019, https://www.fastcompany.
com/90430303/a-rediscovered-1997-video-reveals-why-jeff-bezos-
chose-books-and-not-cds-to-be-amazons-first-product.
4. Thanks to our colleague Jim Guszcza for alerting us to Picard's
conscious choices. See also Raffi Khatchadourian, "We Know
How You Feel," *New Yorker*, January 12, 2015, https://www.
newyorker.com/magazine/2015/01/19/know-feel.
5. On Shake Shack, see Rob Brunner, "How Shake Shack Leads the
Better Burger Revolution," *Fast Company*, June 22, 2015, https://
www.fastcompany.com/3046753/shake-shack-leads-the-better-
burger-revolution; Blue Ocean Team, "How Shake Shack Flipped
the Burger Restaurant: A Case Study," https://www.blueocean-
strategy.com/blog/how-shake-shack-flipped-burger-restaurant-
case-study/.
6. Brunner, "How Shake Shack Leads."
7. Ibid.

CHAPTER 8: DRIVE AND ADAPT: TAKING CONTROL

1. Gym Jones and Bobby have parted ways and the experience at
Gym Jones has shifted considerably.

2. Burton W. Fulsom, "Billy Durant and the Founding of General Motors," Mackinac Center for Public Policy, https://www.mackinac.org/article.aspx?ID=651.

3. The quotation comes from Bill Loomis, "1900–1930: The Years of Driving Dangerously," *Detroit News*, April 26, 2015, https://www.detroitnews.com/story/news/local/michigan-history/2015/04/26/auto-traffic-history-detroit/26312107/.

4. "Durant, William C.," *Encyclopedia of Detroit*: https://detroithistorical.org/learn/encyclopedia-of-detroit/durant-william-c.

5. Yi Wen, "China's Rapid Rise: From Backward Agrarian Society to Industrial Powerhouse in Just 35 Years," St. Louis Fed Working Paper, April 12, 2016, https://www.stlouisfed.org/publications/regional-economist/april-2016/chinas-rapid-rise-from-backward-agrarian-society-to-industrial-powerhouse-in-just-35-years.

6. Echo Huang, "WeChat Is Setting a Blueprint for the World's Social Networks," *Quartz*, October 29, 2019, https://qz.com/1613489/how-wechat-put-the-internet-in-chinas-hands/.

7. Michael R. Wade and Jialu Shan, "The Red Envelope War," IMD Research and Knowledge, April 2016, https://www.imd.org/research-knowledge/articles/the-uneasy-truce-between-alibaba-and-tencent-is-over/; Josh Horwitz, "Over 8 Billion "Red Envelopes" Were Sent over WeChat during Chinese New Year," *Quartz*, February 9, 2016, https://qz.com/613384/over-8-billion-red-envelopes-were-sent-over-wechat-during-chinese-new-year/.

8. "Persistence, Persistence, Persistence: Lessons in Device Innovation from Three Prolific Inventors," *Interventional News*, November 20, 2017, https://interventionalnews.com/persistence-device-innovation/.

9. See *UNIVERSITY OF BRITISH COLUMBIA v CONOR MEDSYSTEMS, INC* [2006] FCAFC 154, Federal Court of Australia, Full Court, 31 October 2006, https://pinpoint.cch.com.au/document/legauUio919065sl49155908/university-of-british-columbia-v-conor-medsystems-inc.

10. See the company fact sheet at https://www.bctechnology.com/companies/Angiotech-Pharmaceuticals-Inc.cfm.

11. Adam Branderberger and Barry Nalebuff, "Inside Intel," *Harvard Business Review*, November–December 1996, https://hbr.org/1996/11/inside-intel.

12. Ian King, "Andy Grove, Valley Veteran Who Founded Intel, Dies at 79," *Bloomberg*, March 21, 2016, https://www.bloomberg.com/news/articles/2016-03-22/andy-grove-taught-silicon-valley-how-to-do-business-dies-at-79.

13. Jan Vrins and Steve Mitnick, "Seven Women CEOs Look Forward," *Public Utilities Fortnightly*, September 2019.

CHAPTER 9: ACTIVATE: HARNESSING YOUR ECOSYSTEM

1. On Pittsburgh, see Simeon Alder, David Lagakos, and Lee Ohanian, "The Decline of the U.S. Rust Belt: A Macroeconomic Analysis," CQER Working Paper 14-05, August 2014, https://www.frbatlanta.org/-/media/Documents/cqer/publications/workingpapers/cqer_wp1405.pdf; David Friedan, "No Light at the End of the Tunnel," *Los Angeles Times*, June 16, 2002, https://www.latimes.com/archives/la-xpm-2002-jun-16-op-friedman-story.html; Dan Bobkoff, "From Stell to Tech, Pittsburgh Transforms Itself," *All Things Considered*, NPR, December 16, 2010, https://www.npr.org/2010/12/16/131907405/from-steel-to-tech-pittsburgh-transforms-itself.

2. For more on ecosystems, see Stuart Crainer, ed., *Ecosystems, Inc.: Understanding, Harnessing, and Developing Organizational Ecosystems* (London: Thinkers50, 2020), which we've drawn on for this chapter.

3. On the history of Mozilla, see Matt Blitz, "Later, Navigator: How Netscape Won and Then Lost the World Wide Web," *Popular Mechanics*, April 4, 2019, https://www.popularmechanics.com/culture/web/a27033147/netscape-navigator-history/; "Mosaic Browser – History of the NCSA Mosaic Internet Web Browser," *The History of the Computer*, https://history-computer.com/Internet/Conquering/Mosaic.html; Matthew Zook, *The Geography of the Internet Industry: Venture Capital, Dot-coms, and Local Knowledge* (New York: Wiley-Blackwell, 2005); John Shinal,

"Netscape: The IPO that Launched at Era," *Marketwatch*, August 5, 2005, https://www.marketwatch.com/story/netscape-ipo-ignited-the-boom-taught-some-hard-lessons-20058518550; Victor Luckerson, "'Crush Them': An Oral History of the Lawsuit That Upended Silicon Valley," *The Ringer*, May 18, 2018, https://www.theringer.com/tech/2018/5/18/17362452/microsoft-antitrust-lawsuit-netscape-internet-explorer-20-years.

4. You can read Raymond's evolving "The Cathedral and the Bazaar" at http://www.catb.org/~esr/writings/cathedral-bazaar/.

5. Jay Hofferman, "The Many Faces (And Names) of Mozilla," *The History of the Web*, February 6, 2017, https://thehistoryoftheweb.com/many-faces-names-mozilla/; see also https://blog.mozilla.org/press/2005/10/firefox-surpasses-100-million-downloads/.

CHAPTER 10: DEBORAH BIAL

1. This quotation comes from a presentation Debbie did at Harvard Business School.

CHAPTER 11: RYAN GRAVEL

1. Bill Torpy, "The Beltline Guy, 20 Years after a Darn Good Term Paper," *Atlanta Journal Constitution*, December 9, 2019, https://www.ajc.com/news/local/torpy-large-the-beltline-guy-years-after-darn-good-term-paper/pcrMCbz69etezThihCVGjN/; Ryan Gravel, *Where We Want to Live: Reclaiming Infrastructure for a New Generation of Cities* (New York: St. Martin's Press, 2016).

2. See https://beltline.org/the-project/project-goals/.

3. "The Simple Ambition of Atlanta's Beltline Project," *Bloomberg CityLab*: https://www.youtube.com/watch?v=s5lL6R91pEA&t=387s.

4. Mark Pendergrast, *City on the Verge: Atlanta and the Fight for America's Urban Future* (New York: Basic Books, 2017); Torpy, "The Beltline Guy." You can read Ryan's thesis, "Belt line – Atlanta: Design of Infrastructure as a Reflection of Public Policy," at https://smartech.gatech.edu/handle/1853/7400.

5. You can access the BeltLine data visualizer at https://garc.maps
   .arcgis.com/apps/webappviewer/index.html?id=af821350e3bc4f3
   abea0b9a3152a7ca1.
6. Claire Marshall, "'Two Simple Rules' Explain Sheepdog Behavior,"
   BBC News, August 27, 2014, https://www.bbc.com/news/science-
   environment-28936251.

CHAPTER 12: VALERIE IRICK RAINFORD

1. Val's framework she uses with client refers to all diverse talent, but
   given the context, Steve associated it with Black talent.

ACKNOWLEDGMENTS

The number of people who touched this book in some way, shape, or form is enormous. We discovered in writing *Detonate* that more input – more voices, more points of view, more dissent over the ideas – will only make the book better. So for everyone who helped us create something that is more interesting than it otherwise would have been, thank you.

Let's start with the person who made it all happen – again – Maeghan Sulham. To say we relied on Maeghan or that she kept us on track is the literal definition of understatement. *Provoke* would not have come to life without Maeghan or at least nowhere nearly as well done or on schedule. That she did this during a time of many complexities in "regular" life makes what she did all the more impressive.

Mike Anderson, Aarushi Uboweja, and Shruti Khullar represent our crack research staff who helped build out the ideas. So many of the great examples in the book came from their keeping a watchful eye on the world to help us illustrate our concepts. We were constantly amazed at how quickly we could tag them with an inquiry on Teams and then receive a range of real-life examples to pick and choose from – as if by magic.

Thank goodness the first cartoonist we contacted to work with us on *Detonate* never returned our email! Thankfully, Maeghan had the good sense to suggest we reach out to Tom and Tallie Fishburne. Tom has once again saved our readers thousands of words (for which we're sure they're thankful!) as he brought some of our ideas to life through illustration. Our working sessions have been so much fun . . . and secretly, we both wish we could draw so we could have a better outlet for our random ideas and observations.

Speaking of saving words, we are grateful for the editorial talent of Tim Sullivan. Tim took our drafts and made them shorter, punchier, and more organized. And everywhere we turn, it seems people know and love Tim. We aren't surprised.

Special thanks go to Jim Guszcza, Deloitte's U.S. chief data scientist, who was especially generous with his time and thinking during the entire process, but especially with Chapters 3 and 4. Jim introduced us to Scott Page, who was kind enough to spend time with us helping bring our own take on his work. Thanks to Scott for brainstorming with us; we hope that we can continue to work together on important issues in the future.

To our provocateurs: Debbie Bial, founder of The Posse Foundation and enabler of a new face of leadership in America; Ryan Gravel, founder of Sixpitch, Generator, Aftercar, and Elevator, and the visionary behind the Atlanta Beltline; and Valerie Rainford, founder of Elloree Talent Strategies, and corporate trailblazer and driver of talent system diversity – thank you for allowing us to share your stories with the world. We are grateful to have been able to get to know each of you and your amazing stories in more detail.

A handful of people offered to do a detailed, advance review of *Provoke*, and we are very thankful for their words of advice and encouragement. Thanks to Dan Helfrich for the coaching; his suggestions made our stories tighter and better. Thanks to Jonathan Goodman for finding places in the book where we could better tie ideas together. Thanks to Kat Jiwani for the myriad ways she made the book clearer throughout. Thanks to Lisa Iliff for her continued support of our work, and patience to work through those early drafts. We particularly appreciate her courage in raising tough issues in such a productive way. And to Tim Tuff and Rider Tuff, thanks for being volunteer copy editors; we understand and applaud their desire to protect the good family name.

During our exploratory process, we were thrilled to have such great input from friends and colleagues who helped shape our thinking, including Chip Bergh, Ambar Chowdhury, Tom Fezza, Sheryl Jacobson, Steve Jennings, Ralph Judah, Tom Fezza, Kwasi Mitchell, Rich Nanda, Phebe Port, Michael Raynor, Jim Stengel, and Max Weise.

We are grateful to the leaders who provided uplifting encouragement throughout the writing process and beyond, including Jason Girzadas, Stacy Janiak, Alicia Rose, Pete Shimer and, of course, Janet Foutty and Joe Ucuzoglu. Thank you for giving us the space to create.

The creation stage is one thing. We have also learned that it takes a village to make sure our book is heard about and enjoyed by many. To our marketing/PR team – Suzanne Kounkel, Kimberly McNeil-Downs, Karen Miklic, and Kelly Nelson, along with Lisa Barnes and Mark Fortier – thanks for helping us spread the word. To our team at Wiley, Richard Narramore and Victoria Anllo, thank you for being so flexible and accommodating.

Farin Clementine and Colleen Lemay make sure we are organized, protect our writing time, and find time for the really important things when we need to show up (or Zoom). We are very thankful for their perseverance and support . . . and always with a smile . . . even virtually.

Finally, we would like to thank the Tuff and Goldbach households for putting up with us as we wrote this entirely at home. We know we are both "a lot to handle" (according to one of you).

From Geoff: Martha, as anyone who knows you – and us – knows, your patience is clearly close to godliness. Rider, Quinn,

Mason, and Hunter – thanks for increasingly taking on the role of people I like to hang out with rather than (just) people I need to parent. You were always there to help me blow off steam!

From Steve: Michelle Dunstan, thank you for understanding when I said I needed to find space to write. Amanda Poulin, thank you for being a terrific teacher to Grayson and putting up with me during the pandemic; you gave us comfort knowing that there was normalcy in at least one part of our lives. And to Grayson Dunstan Goldbach, thanks for constantly asking Alexa and Google how to say *Provoke* in Chinese.

ABOUT THE AUTHORS

Geoff Tuff is a principal at Deloitte, where he holds a variety of leadership roles across its sustainability, innovation, and strategy practices. In the past, he led Doblin, the firm's innovation practice, and was a senior partner at Monitor Group, serving as a member of its global board of directors before Deloitte acquired the company. He has been with some form of Monitor Group for close to 30 years.

Geoff's work centers around helping clients transform their businesses to grow and compete in nontraditional ways. Over the course of his career, Geoff has worked in virtually every industry and he uses that breadth of experience to bring novel insights about how things might operate to clients stuck in industry conventional wisdom.

Geoff is valued for his integrative approach to solving problems. He combines deep analytic and strategic expertise with a natural orientation toward approaches embodied in design thinking. He is a frequent speaker and writer on the topic of growth through innovation and has written for a variety of outlets, including *Harvard Business Review*. Geoff holds degrees from Dartmouth College and Harvard Business School.

Steven Goldbach is a principal at Deloitte and serves the U.S. partnership as the firm's chief strategy officer. Prior to joining Deloitte, Steve was a partner at Monitor Group and head of its New York office and head of strategy at *Forbes*.

Steve helps executives and their teams transform their organizations by making challenging and pragmatic strategy choices in the face of uncertainty. He is an architect, expert practitioner, and teacher of the variety of strategy methodologies developed and practiced by Monitor Deloitte over the years. He focuses his work on clients and industries undergoing large-scale transformation. Steve helps companies combine rigor and creativity to create their own future.

Steve holds degrees from Queen's University at Kingston and Columbia Business School.

Geoff and Steve's 2018 book, *Detonate: Why – and How – Corporations Must Blow Up Best Practices (and bring a beginner's mind) to Survive*, became a national bestseller and led to Geoff and Steve's short-listing for the 2019 Thinkers50 Distinguished Achievement Award in Strategy.

INDEX